Warren Buffett

The Motley Fool

WARREN BUFFETT INVESTS LIKE A GIRL

AND WHY YOU SHOULD, TOO

LOUANN LOFTON

with a foreword by Tom Gardner

HARPER
BUSINESS

An Imprint of HarperCollins*Publishers*
www.harpercollins.com

A hardcover edition of this book was published in 2011 by Harper Business, an imprint of HarperCollins Publishers.

FIRST HARPER BUSINESS PAPERBACK EDITION PUBLISHED 2012

Designed by Fritz Metsch

The Library of Congress has cataloged the hardcover edition as follows:

Lofton, LouAnn
Warren Buffett invests like a girl: and why you should too / LouAnn Lofton, with a forward by Tom Gardner.
p.cm.
Summary: "Investing isn't a man's world anymore—and this book shows why that's a good thing for individual portfolios, Wall Street, and the world's financial system"—Provided by publisher.
ISBN 98-0-06-156755-1 (hardcover)
1. Investments—Psychological aspects. 2. Portfolio management—Psychological aspects. 3. Speculation—Psychological aspects. I. Title
HG4515.15.L64 2011
332.6—dc22   2011013590

ISBN 978-0-06-172763-4 (pbk.)

HB 09.18.2023

Dedicated to my mother and to the memory of my father

Contents

Foreword

This is a book for investors about investing. It focuses on the factors that will best determine if you will make or lose money, and whether you'll beat the market.

You might naturally assume, then, that you'll be reading about how to pick stocks—so that you buy GEICO instead of Bank of America. How to evaluate a company's profitability—so that you invest in Steve Jobs' Apple, not Donald Trump's Trump Entertainment Resorts. How to dig deep into a financial statement. How to find the next company poised to rise 10, 20, or 100 times in value.

But, no.

Instead, this book will analyze what will make or break your performance as an investor—your brain, your emotions, your personality. If you harness them, your investment returns will lead you to financial freedom in the Foolish fields of opportunity. But if they harness you, close your eyes because the chili won't stop hitting the fan. You'll sell when you should've been buying. You'll believe what you should have doubted. You'll shout while you should've been learning. You'll trade when you should always have been investing.

If you want to sustainably make more and more money in the market—using common stocks or mutual funds—you'll have to learn how to master your temperament. A fine place to start is here, in these pages, as LouAnn Lofton reveals how Warren Buffett parlayed the small investments of a teenager into the largest and greatest investment portfolio in human history.

It's a worthwhile case study!

But up until now, the master's students have looked for his virtuosity mostly in the wrong places. They've dreamed in complex variables while trying to unearth Buffett's valuation models. They've quizzed the inner circles of his inner circle and, without discretion, have rooted through the most personal material of his life. They've spent decades overlooking what matters most but, hey, at least they've tried!

Over on Wall Street, at the desks of macho traders and salesmen, they ignore Buffett. These guys have done their best to take the Triple Crown: (1) destroying investor portfolios, (2) sinking the balance sheets of their employers, and (3) leveling the world economy. And they've done it all in the name of big commission-driven bonuses. Their game is not about investing, it's about scalping profit while you take all the risk.

If you want to know how to make millions investing in stocks, just do the exact opposite of what's on offer in the high-octane world of Wall Street, where men will be men, right up until they ask taxpayers to bail them out. Turn the page, dear Fool, and you will see what most of the world has overlooked or ignored. It's simple, really: Warren Buffett invests like a girl.

—*Tom Gardner, December 2010*

Warren Buffett Invests Like a Girl

I

Why Temperament Matters Now
More Than Ever

September 2008. Britney Spears prepped for a triumphant
return to MTV's Video Music Awards, following a lackluster
2007 VMA performance. Cyclist Lance Armstrong announced
he'd come out of retirement to compete in the next Tour de
France. Hurricane Ike had become the fifth hurricane of the
Atlantic hurricane season. Delegates at the Republican National Convention named Arizona senator John McCain as
their candidate for the November presidential elections. Actor
Mickey Rourke was back in the spotlight thanks to the movie
The Wrestler, which picked up the award for best film at the
Venice Film Festival. Roger Federer won an astonishing fifth
consecutive tennis title at the U.S. Open, while Serena Williams picked up her third overall, and first since 2002. British rapper M.I.A. had a hit on her hands with "Paper Planes,"
as did Atlanta's own T.I. with "Whatever You Like." Fans
of NBC's *The Office* eagerly awaited the premiere of the fifth
season to see what kind of hijinks would ensue with Michael
Scott and the rest of the Dunder Mifflin team. The defending
Super Bowl champion New York Giants beat the Washington
Redskins 16–7 in the NFL's season opener.

Then, less than two weeks into the month, the world changed. Forever.

A financial panic engulfed stock markets, individual investors, and world governments alike. And *panic* was indeed the perfect word for what happened in the fall of 2008. Writing in the nineteenth century about market panics, Yale professor William Graham Sumner defined one as "a wave of emotion, apprehension, alarm. It is more or less irrational. It is superinduced upon a crisis, which is real and inevitable, but it exaggerates, conjures up possibilities, takes away courage and energy."[1]

We'd seen a preview of this madness earlier that same year, as escalating leverage and a slowing housing market crippled debt-rich companies like investment banking firm Bear Stearns, which was forced to sell itself under much duress to JP Morgan (which had the backing and support of the federal government for the purchase) in March 2008 for a bargain price.[2] The housing boom, fueled by subprime borrowing and backed by banks and Wall Street companies looking to cash in on it, began to unravel. And as it did so, it quickly became clear that the credit markets, and the balance sheets of just about every bank and financial firm under the sun and moon, were filled with horrid loads of bad debt. Indeed, it was a "real and inevitable" crisis.

Bear Stearns' demise spooked the market and investors in March. The world then watched as one troubled bank and hedge fund after another revealed that they, too, were suffering under the weight of bad loans, leading us limping into September, when the bankruptcy filing of the storied and debt-laden financial firm Lehman Brothers (the government refused to step in here as they had with Bear to make sure a sale of the firm happened) sent the markets over a cliff. The credit markets, both between businesses and between businesses and individuals, ground to a halt. No one knew who was hiding what in their financial statements. No one knew which balance sheets you could trust, and which you couldn't. It seemed safer to assume the worst, and it seems that's what just about everybody did.

As one famous sage has said, "You only learn who has been swimming naked when the tide goes out."[3] In the fall of 2008, Wall Street was a virtual nudist colony. And people, it wasn't pretty, as if I need to remind you.

Stock markets dropped dramatically, leaving investors to hang on for dear life. Volatility was the word of the day, with the so-called "fear index" reaching new heights as the markets reached new lows. Consumer confidence and investor sentiment plummeted right alongside stock prices. The very future of the economy was uncertain from one minute to the next, with one established financial company after another at a precipice, dangling over the edge, not sure what was ahead.

Hello, panic.

By October 6, 2008, the Dow Jones Industrial Average fell below 10,000 points for the first time since 2004. Three days later, it would drop below 8,600. That same day, October 9, the Standard & Poor's 500 index (which tracks 500 of the largest companies in the United States) marked a 42 percent decline over the past year, easily wiping away gains that had taken years to build. This milestone came less than four short, painful weeks after the Lehman Brothers bankruptcy.

It was a time that tested the mettle and tried the nerves of even the most seasoned investor. I watched, wide-eyed and with no small amount of horror, as my portfolio (containing, in some cases, shares of companies I'd owned for more than ten years) shrank to just a wisp of itself. How low could it ultimately go? Well-run companies that had nothing to do with the banks' or financial institutions' troubles were slaughtered right alongside them. You would have thought popular consumer brand and retail companies had suddenly started dabbling in mortgage-backed securities versus selling their soft drinks and leggings.

Flipping on the television each morning became an act of desperation and adventure, in a strange sense. I felt compelled to look, to see what had happened overnight, to see what new fresh awful thing was going to be inflicted on us that day. To compare it to a car wreck, where you honestly don't want to look because you fear what you'll see, but you seem unable not to, is apt.

Only in this case, there's a crucial difference: We were all in this car together as it crashed, leaving us in a mangled heap.

The hair-raising drops and sheer panic had breathless commentators struggling to keep up. News was breaking so fast, it was nearly impossible to know the latest, most up-to-date information. Important people in fancy cars and fancier suits in places like Manhattan, Washington, D.C., and London were coming and going from meetings, their entries and exits broadcast on television as if they were celebrities. (Meanwhile, Britney did just fine at the VMAs, second time around, thank you very much.)

Through it all, a man sat far removed from the hubbub of New York City and Washington, D.C., in the Midwest, in quiet, placid Omaha, Nebraska. He watched, as he'd watched so many times before, as the world was seemingly coming to an end. He heard the shrill voices on TV and even he probably couldn't escape the daily, even hourly, deluge of photographs of Wall Street traders looking horrified, frazzled, or just plain resigned to it all.

Then, he did what any rational person should have done in the face of so much fear. He took a deep breath, steadied himself, and started buying stocks, putting $20 billion to work in companies like Goldman Sachs and General Electric. It took courage, fortitude, and an ability to look past the current crisis to the eventual recovery of American businesses and the world economy.

It took the right temperament. Warren Buffett, our man in Omaha (and the "famous sage" quoted earlier), didn't panic and sell. He remained calm, and he assessed the situation. And when he did, he acted from a place of certitude, backed up by years of experience. He encouraged others to do the same, reminding them that we'd been through tough times before and we'd come out ahead each time. He also reminded investors that the best time to buy stocks was when everyone was fleeing the market, leaving bargains galore ready for the taking.

To say that this was an easy mindset to adopt during this frenzied time period is an understatement of colossal proportions. It's demoralizing to watch your 401(k) grow smaller by the day, by the hour even, for weeks on end. It's exhausting and incredibly disheartening to watch your nest egg, your retirement account, or the kids' college fund all evaporate. It's like we were all just being beat over the head repeatedly and we couldn't escape it. The hits, they just kept coming and coming.

I managed to buck up and actually buy some more shares of a few companies I already owned on the Tuesday after Lehman filed for bankruptcy. And I am not exaggerating when I say that was one of the hardest things in investing I'd ever done. Actually making that decision, that choice to willingly push myself back into a market that was already, even at that early stage, leaving me bloodied and bruised, was so difficult. It was a scary time and it took every ounce of willpower I had to click the little "buy" button on my broker's website. Everything in my body was telling me not to. Luckily, my head knew better and overruled the stark fear coursing through me.

Once I bought those shares, though, the pain really began. I had no idea that weeks and months of a whipsawing market lay ahead of me, testing my ability to hunker down and hold on. I never sold, though. I waited it out. And now, looking at the returns on two of the three stocks I bought more of that day (Apple Computer and Chipotle Mexican Grill), I'm happy I did. As for the third? Well, they can't all be winners now, can they? (Cough, Chesapeake Energy, cough.)

Warren Buffett has built a long and enviable career in the financial business, with a track record most investors and money managers can only dream of (and would probably kill for). For nearly five decades, he's been analyzing companies, investing in the best of them, and building wealth. He is absolutely without parallel. His ability to pick stocks and invest in companies that profit and endure is next to none. And yet what truly defines Buffett, what makes him the investor he is today, what separates him from everyone else, from all those other investors over the years, is his remarkable temperament.

The *American Heritage Dictionary* defines *temperament* as "the manner of thinking, behaving, or reacting characteristic of a particular person."[4] In the world of investing, temperament manifests itself in whether you are ruled by emotions when you make decisions, causing you, for example, to buy and then freak out and sell before you should. Whether you take on too much risk. Whether you're frenetically moving into and out of stocks without ever having a clue as to what the business behind them actually does. Whether you let yourself get rattled by market movements to a paralyzing point, or whether you look at declining prices and see opportunities.

Buffett himself has talked about the importance of temperament, saying, "The most important quality for an investor is temperament, not intellect. . . . You need a temperament that neither derives great pleasure from being with the crowd or against the crowd."[5]

He's also said, "Success in investing doesn't correlate with IQ once you're above the level of 125. Once you have ordinary intelligence, what you need is the temperament to control the urges that get other people into trouble in investing."[6]

Talk about "trouble," indeed. We can surely point to temperament—the wrong kind, that is—when looking for some of the root causes of the financial crisis:

- Short-term thinking in abundance
- Risk taking in ridiculous excess
- Debt levels that were completely beyond reason
- The irrational belief that the greed-filled moneymaking wouldn't stop anytime soon
- The inability to see the long-term consequences of such poor decision making
- The cynical profiteering off the next rube around the corner

So long as there was someone foolish enough to sell to at an ever-higher price, whether we're talking houses or stocks or packages of subprime loans couched as safe investments, the raucous party just kept on going.

Now, granted, lots of other factors were also in play here, leading up to the financial crisis. We can't blame it fully and solely on temperament. It's an enormously complex situation that built up over years and years. Incentives played a significant role, as did the regulatory environment and loose monetary policy. Competition among Wall Street firms was so fierce that in order to just keep up with one another, traders and financiers increasingly were unable to say no to anything. If a firm didn't want to handle a deal because it was worried it would turn out badly, there was always another place down the street that would. However, temperament did indeed have a role.

Looking back, faulty temperaments can be discovered at all levels of the unfolding crisis, starting with those folks looking for a slice of the American dream: the homebuyers themselves. Now, of course, there *were* responsible people who somehow got ensnared in the subprime mess, or worse yet, were tricked into taking on loans they never had a solid chance of actually making good on. But many folks deliberately took on extreme amounts of debt to buy more house than they needed or could afford (and, in some cases, more *houses* than they needed or could afford), often in the form of interest-only or adjustable rate mortgages, or sometimes combinations of both. It was known that these mortgages would eventually reset, possibly at much higher rates, meaning the payments on them could rise dramatically. The hope for many taking on this risk was that the housing bubble would continue to inflate without pause, and that home values would continue to rise into the stratosphere, allowing a safe, swift exit before the mortgage rate reset became an issue.

Alas, it was not to be.

Home values started to tumble, mortgages began to reset at untenable rates, and eventually the monthly interest payments started choking those who had so enthusiastically taken them on in the first place. Missed payments led to defaults and bad debt began to rise. This growing trend suffocated homeowners, then the banks and financial institutions, then the credit markets and stock market both here and worldwide, infecting the global economy from the ground up. And all because not enough people realized that long-term thinking and prudent risk taking are virtues, not curses.

On the other side of the aisle stood the bankers and the financial institutions—the titans of Wall Street—dirtied with even more temperamental filth than the shortsighted homebuyer. They may not have been the ones taking out the subprime loans, but they sure were minting a profit from them and encouraging the irrational behavior behind them to continue. And thanks to their willingness to leverage themselves at levels no reasonable person could ever support or understand, or hardly even fathom, they then spread the problems created by a collapsing housing market far and wide.

Questions began to arise about how reliable and solid the collateral of any bank actually was, since everyone had this toxic stuff on their books. That's what caused the credit markets to start seizing up. No banks wanted to lend to one another, because they couldn't trust that the counterparty would actually be able to pay them back. They couldn't trust that their books didn't hide dirty secrets like everyone else's did.

When lending nearly stopped between financial institutions, individuals weren't far behind.

Panic, our old friend.

Once again, we see temperament at the scene of the crime. The wrong temperament was pervasive on Wall Street and was like gasoline on a fire. Any sense of acceptable risk went right out the window, as the money kept pouring in. The culture of the day became overburdened with macho, me-first, make-money-no-matter-what cutthroat attitudes. Traders were making millions thanks to massive overleveraging and ever more complex derivatives, many of which were based on not much more than lies. Risk taking, a lack of consequences, and short-term thinking ruled the day.

Even most of the very people propelling the mess forward knew it wouldn't last forever. It simply couldn't. But instead of realizing that the good times wouldn't last and taking smart steps to invest with a longer-term outlook, the overriding reaction by most of the players was to just get as much as they could while they could—who cared about the consequences?

Not only was flawed temperament to blame in part, then, for the unfolding credit crisis, thanks both to homebuyers taking on too much debt and Wall Street following behind, doing the same, eager to make a quick buck, but it also made the resultant financial panic that much more pronounced. The stock market dropped, investors fled, cashing out their stocks at the absolute worst time; the stock market dropped again, investors fled . . . Lather, rinse, repeat. Meanwhile, Buffett sat calmly, waiting to make his move, waiting to buy shares of good companies at attractive prices, a very model of the right temperament—that of an investor and not a speculator.

Here's the good news for us—we can learn to adopt a more

long-term-focused temperament. We can become calmer investors. We can shift ourselves from speculators to an investment mindset. We can tamp down our risk taking. And if we don't ever want to see the mistakes of the financial crisis and panic of 2008 repeated again, it seems smart to do so.

Your own investment results will improve as you learn to control your emotions and adopt a Buffett-like temperament. We might not be able to get every person working on Wall Street to focus on improving their temperaments, although that would undoubtedly make our financial system stronger and less erratic, but we can start here, with each other, with our own behavior.

Now, here's where things get even more interesting, for at least one segment of readers and investors. We can all work to improve our temperaments, yes, but one group in particular needs to work a bit harder to do so. And they're the ones who need it the most.

Men, I'm looking at you.

It must be said that the majority of traders on Wall Street, the majority of board members at financial companies, and the majority of executives at investment banks share one very notable quality—a Y chromosome. Wall Street, at least at the top, at least when it comes to decision making and the power to affect things, is still a boys' club.[7] And while homebuyers, both male and female, share the blame for the financial crisis, it was primarily men running the big money on Wall Street who exported the problem and made the situation exponentially worse.

Sure, there were a handful of women to be found on Wall Street in positions of power. Erin Callan, chief financial officer at Lehman Brothers in the heady summer of 2008, comes to mind (although it must be pointed out that she came into that position in September 2007, well after a big chunk of the leverage at the firm had been piled on).[8] But by and large, it was, and it remains, a man's world

So-called "feminine" qualities like relationship building, patience, and collaboration were markedly absent during the most recent market mania. Had there been more of that temperament around Wall Street, and indeed more women on the trading floors and in the boardrooms, it's possible things wouldn't have turned out as they did. And if things hadn't turned out as they did, we would all have larger portfolios and fewer sleepless nights by this point.

Men, you've got some 'splainin' to do.

Studies have shown that women have a different approach to investing than men do. They think long-term and don't trade as much. They eschew risk more than men do. They're better able to think for themselves and not bend to peer pressure. And they have much less testosterone, which affects markets in ways we are still discovering, thanks to new developments in the field of neuroeconomics. The way that women tend to approach investing is healthier and calmer, and it's the way we should all approach investing, both men and women alike.

THE CURIOUS CASE OF ICELAND

Lots of weird things went down during the panic of 2008, but perhaps none was as strange as what happened in the tiny nation of Iceland. The country, just 300,000 citizens strong, saw itself transformed, nearly overnight, from a small, humble fishing nation into a hotbed of international financial activity. Former fishermen were trading derivatives, something they'd probably never even heard of before 2003. The country's debt got so out of hand that at one point it was an astonishing 850 percent of its gross domestic product.[9] Risk taking in excess, carried out largely by aggressive male bankers, drove this little country virtually straight into bankruptcy, with nothing but a collapsed currency and dashed dreams to show for their trouble.

So, who was called in to save the day? Yes, women. To correct course, female Icelandic politicians, bankers, and business minds took charge of the country's faltering economy. A female prime minister was elected, and women in prominent financial positions found new audiences among frustrated Icelanders eager for change.

Most notable among them are Halla Tómasdóttir and Kristin Petursdóttir, who together founded Audur Capital in 2007, before the economy there went to pieces. Their company was founded on "feminine values" and survived the Icelandic financial crisis intact—a real feat, looking at the financial landscape there today.

Tómasdóttir described her thinking, and Audur's values, in a February 2009 article:[10]

"We have five core feminine values. First, risk awareness: we will not invest in things we don't understand. Second, profit with principles—we like a wider definition so it is not just economic profit, but a positive social and environmental impact. Third, emotional capital. When we invest, we do an emotional due diligence—or check on the company—we look at the people, at whether the corporate culture is an asset or a liability. Fourth, straight talking. We believe the language of finance should be accessible, and not part of the alienating nature of banking culture. Fifth, independence. We would like to see women increasingly financially independent, because with that comes the greatest freedom to be who you want to be, but also unbiased advice."

The story of Iceland is still unfolding, as the country's financial woes continue to haunt it years later. It finally emerged from the 2008 recession in the third quarter of 2010, though its troubles aren't completely over.[11] But could this tiny nation lead the way into a more enlightened financial future for the world economy? One can only hope.

Luckily for all of us, we have an outstanding model to guide us in the search for the desired investing temperament: Warren Buffett. When compared to the research on men's and women's investing styles, and the differences between them, Buffett's investment style looks very similar to those strategies employed by women. His temperament, that which defines him and makes him the master investor he is, is more feminine, if you will, than masculine.

And if there's any doubt as to the validity of this style and temperament versus something a bit more, say, macho, allow me to point you in the direction of his returns versus those of the investment houses on Wall Street in 2008 and beyond. Buffett's been Buffett for decades, building his wealth over time, while the boys on Wall Street destroyed theirs—and ours, too!—in just several short months. Buffett's compounded annual book value gain has been more than double the return of the S&P 500 for more than forty years, while they dashed our 401(k)s and sent the economy into a spiral.

There can be no question as to which is the more sustainable path, which is the smartest way to create wealth over the long term, which is the best way for us—for *all* of us—to invest for a bright future. It's time for a change. It's time to embrace the feminine.

It's time, quite simply, for all of us to invest like girls, right alongside the greatest investor of all time, Warren Buffett.

So, here's how things will go from here. We'll start with

a look at the research on the topic of women and investing. (You didn't think we'd let that just slide, did you?) From there we'll spend a chunk of time looking at how Warren Buffett exemplifies the ideal, feminine investing temperament. We'll then learn some Foolish investment tenets to help you on your way to becoming an investor, or to improving your current investment returns if you're already investing on your own. And we'll close with appendices that are not to be missed: interviews with several investors who are models of temperament themselves, along with a recap of what we learned, and a reading list for those of you who want to learn even more.

So, gather your things, get comfortable, grab a drink, and settle in. Once you're done reading this book, you will be ready to invest with a temperament that will help you be successful. Oh, and you'll have fun along the way. Investing *should* be fun, after all. Buffett himself says he tap-dances to work each morning. By the end of this, you'll be tap-dancing, too.

2

The Science Behind the Girl

Following the financial crisis and panic of 2008, the role and influence of men in our economy appears to be shrinking just at the time that women's role and influence is expanding. Men were, by and large, much more affected by job losses in the recent recession. A look at the industries at the root of the problem—housing/construction and finance—explains why. Women now actually make up the majority of the United States' workforce, marking the first time in our country's history that that's been the case.[1]

More women are also becoming more educated, with women earning almost 60 percent of undergraduate degrees. That same percentage, 60 percent, holds for master's degrees as well.[2] And for the first time ever, women narrowly edged out men in earning PhDs in the 2008–2009 academic year.[3] It's safe to say, then, that women, more than men, are equipping themselves to thrive and prosper in today's economy and beyond.

Will we see women taking over more financial jobs, too? It's possible. Women currently earn 42 percent of the country's MBAs.[4] And looking at the overall shift that seems to be taking hold after the crisis, and the increased value that will continue (hopefully) to be placed on calmer temperaments, it's probable that more women will gravitate to Wall Street.

So then, if we believe that men and women adopting a more "feminine" attitude toward investing could change the world of finance for the better, and at the same time fatten our individual brokerage accounts (it's not all about mere philosophizing here), we'd better back up our claims, right? After all, basing our assumptions on so-called "female intuition" would be downright sexist.

Lucky for us, academic researchers and behavioral economists have been putting in the long hours and hard work necessary to tease out the differences between how men invest and how women invest. The studies and surveys go back years and cover nearly every aspect of investing—decision making, risk assessment, trading frequency, and consistency of results, just to name a few.

Researchers have also studied the differences among professional investors, both male and female, highlighting the fact that these variations in temperament aren't limited just to the universe of the individual investor. And some of the most interesting recent studies have just begun to uncover the role of testosterone in investing, risk taking, and trading. You're not shocked to hear it has one, are you?

▦ GIRLS WILL BE GIRLS

Brad M. Barber and Terrance Odean of the University of California (Davis and Berkeley campuses, respectively) published what is likely the most famous (or infamous, in some circles) and groundbreaking study on gender differences in investing with their February 2001 *Quarterly Journal of Economics* paper, "Boys Will Be Boys: Gender, Overconfidence, and Common Stock Investment."[5] (Gotta love that title, right?)

By surveying 35,000 discount brokerage accounts over a nearly six-year period, Barber and Odean found several distinct differences both in temperament and performance for men versus women. Their paper was predicated on prior research, which had shown that men tend to be more overconfident than women in so-called "manly" pursuits (of which, we can still, sadly but not surprisingly, count finance). Put simply, men think they know more than they do. Women are more willing to admit that they know what they don't know. They're more willing to own up to the fact that they don't know everything.

So, how does the issue of overconfidence play into investing behavior and results? Well, because of their overconfidence, it was assumed—correctly, as it turned out—that men would trade more than women do. And what does more frequent trading do to your investment results? It drags them down, running up transaction costs and acting like the proverbial albatross on what might otherwise be smart investment decisions.

Barber and Odean found that men traded the stocks (also known as "securities") in their accounts 45 percent more than women did. Forty-five percent! This excessive flip-flopping of securities reduced their net returns by 2.65 percentage points, compared to the 1.72 percentage points women dinged their accounts by trading. Single men were even worse offenders, trading 67 percent more than single women.

Married men fared worse than married women, but they weren't as bad off as the single guys. This wasn't surprising to Barber and Odean, given everything they knew about overconfidence studies. It's possible that wives were influencing their husbands here, helping them tone down their overconfidence, and that in turn helped their investment returns.

Now, it should be noted that Barber and Odean found that both sexes hurt themselves by trading too frequently—men just hurt themselves more. Unnecessary trading is the real devil here.

Here's where one of the most interesting outcomes from Barber and Odean comes into play for our purposes—women's outperformance over the men wasn't related to better stock picking or to market timing. It wasn't that women were finding the perfect stocks at the perfect time. Barber and Odean emphasize this again and again in their paper.

The key here is that women's trading hurt their performance less than men's, thanks to men's greater overconfidence. The difference, then, is more related to temperament than it is to skill. You can be the smartest securities analyst around, but not having the correct mindset can absolutely sink you as an investor. All the know-how in the world can't correct for bad habits. Temperament matters, plain and simple.

Barber and Odean also pioneered the insight that "women tend to hold less risky positions than men in their common stock portfolios." Prior social science research had shown that women, on average, are more risk averse than men, but this (according to the authors themselves) was the first bit of documented evidence that women were choosing safer securities than men were.

The study measured "risk" for the investors' portfolios multiple ways (we can boil it down to "volatility" for our purposes here), and across them all, men exposed themselves to more risk than women did, with (who else?) single men exposing themselves to the most. Higher risk exposure *should* result in higher returns—that's what compensates investors for taking it, after all. If you didn't think you'd be rewarded for forgoing a sure thing for a less sure thing, you wouldn't do it, right?

But here that's not the case. Despite their willingness to go for risk with gusto, the male investors in Barber and Odean's study simply traded their profits away. Once again, we're face-to-face with temperament.

So from Barber and Odean we can see that because men are overconfident they trade more (much more) than women do, and as a result, women's returns are higher. We also have learned that women tend to hold less risky securities than men do. Trade less, while taking less risk. So far, score two for the gentler sex.

■ **TAKE THE MONEY AND RUN**

Mutual fund powerhouse Vanguard analyzed the movements in 2.7 million of its investors' IRA accounts during the financial panic of 2008 and 2009, and what they found shouldn't surprise anyone who knows about Barber and Odean's results.[6]

Yes indeed, women were more likely than men to stay put during the herky-jerky market antics, not touching their portfolios. More men tended to freak out and sell their stocks right at precisely the wrong time—the bottom. They locked in undoubtedly huge losses, and on the flip side likely missed out on the market's recovery as well. Men's overconfidence apparently led them to trade when they shouldn't have, when the best course of action would have been to stand pat.

Remember the harrowing scenes I described in chapter 1,

with the market collapsing all around us? It was a difficult time to be steady and do the right thing, which was, of course, *to not sell*. The ability to be calm and not make rash decisions in the face of such chaos is an incredibly important characteristic of successful investors over the long term. It's also one of the most difficult to master. At the time, it feels like absolute hell. Trust me, I remember how it was that fall. I remember my stomach turning, watching as my portfolio got redder and redder day by day. But I also knew that I'd feel worse whenever the world finally stopped ending if I'd thrown my hands up in the air and sold everything, versus just taking a deep breath and being still. Based on Vanguard's data at least, it appears that in this most recent investment storm, women, more than men, demonstrated this vital ability to be patient and wait it out.

■ WHEN OPTIMISM ISN'T OPTIMAL

So far we've learned that women tend to trade less than men, take less risk, and are more likely not to sell at the worst possible time. Now we'll look at a positive aspect of pessimism, as counterintuitive as that might sound.

In her paper "Female Investors and Securities Fraud: Is the Reasonable Investor a Woman?" Joan MacLeod Heminway of the University of Tennessee College of Law presents a concise history of much of the research on male versus female investing habits.[7] One interesting point she highlights is that female investors may be less optimistic than male investors—and I think that's a good thing.

While optimism in most parts of our lives is something to strive for, in investing it can poison your judgment and outlook. Optimists tend to overstate their abilities and investment acumen (hello "overconfidence" from Barber and Odean), take more risks, and can sometimes pay attention only to information that is positive and supports conclusions they've already come to. Because of their sunny outlook, they tend to assume only the best can happen to their stocks, and they don't want to hear otherwise.

Pessimists, on the other hand, tend to be more realistic, and in investing, clear-eyed realism beats pie-in-the-sky optimism any day of the week. Women, thanks partly to the fact that they lack the same confidence levels as men, and also rate their investing knowledge below what men believe about their own investing skill, tend to react more realistically. They're better judges about their potential returns and abilities, even if that means they tend to doubt themselves more. Overconfidence and optimism can kill returns, so in this case, a little self-doubt can actually work in women's favor.

■ GIRLS JUST WANT TO HAVE FUNDS

We know now that female individual investors tend to be less optimistic, are less likely to panic and sell when the market's crashing around them, and tend to trade less and take less risk. But what about professional investors who happen to be women? Do these differences still hold?

Stefan Ruenzi and Alexandra Niessen conducted a study on the differences between male and female mutual fund managers that verified some past findings and uncovered new ones.[8] The pair analyzed returns for all U.S. mutual funds run by individuals (versus teams) for the period from January 1994 to December 2006. In the end, the authors studied 15,170 funds; about 10 percent of those were managed by women. While the differences for this subset of investors weren't as pronounced as they were for retail (or individual) investors, they nonetheless highlighted key temperament advantages for women.

Again, female investors were shown to be more risk averse than male investors. The new spin here is that the female fund managers chose to invest using "significantly less extreme investment styles" than did the male managers. Not only that, but women stuck to their investment guns more than men; they didn't see a need to be changing up investment styles willy-nilly. And once again, female investors traded less frequently than males did. Yes, even among professionals, that difference still held.

What's interesting here, however, is that there was *not* a performance advantage for women over men thanks to their calm, patient temperaments. Performance between the two groups was about equal. But performance isn't everything. Consistency and "performance persistence" (or the ability to generate steady returns year after year) matter, too.

Ruenzi and Niessen demonstrated that thanks to staying true to their investment process and philosophy and not switching up investment styles to chase the next hot thing, and thanks to their seemingly natural willingness to invest using "less extreme investment styles," the female-managed mutual funds in the study achieved more consistent returns with more persistent performance. In short, there were fewer wild performance swings in the female-managed funds than in the male-managed funds. To quote the study's authors, "These findings show that past performance is a better indicator of future performance for female managed funds than for male managed funds."[9]

While there may not have been significant performance

differences between male and female mutual fund managers, recent statistics about hedge fund managers reveal exactly the opposite. A hedge fund is a special type of investment fund available almost exclusively to high-net-worth individuals and institutional investors. Typically, the managers of the funds "hedge" positions within their portfolios, going both long and short stocks (that is, they are betting that some stocks will go up in value and some will go down). In many cases, a hedge fund can be riskier than your average mutual fund.

Hedge Fund Research, Inc., a source of information and data on the hedge fund industry, tracked the annualized performance of female-managed hedge funds from 2000 to May 2009.[10] They discovered that funds managed by women have, since inception, returned an average 9.06 percent, compared to just 5.82 percent averaged by a weighted index of other hedge funds. As if that outperformance weren't impressive enough, the group also found that during the financial panic of 2008, these women-managed funds weren't hurt nearly as severely as the rest of the hedge fund universe, with the funds dropping 9.61 percent compared to the 19.03 percent suffered by other funds. So, they performed better on the upside and lost less on the downside. While this study didn't get into the particulars of the reasons for this superior performance, we can take a guess that it probably had something to do with what we've seen in the other studies.

■ **PUTTING PEER PRESSURE IN ITS PLACE**

All right, so far we've built an image in our heads of the female investor as one who takes less risk, trades less, tends to be more realistic, and withstands whipsawing markets better than male investors. We've also learned that female investors tend to produce results that are more consistent, and in the hedge fund world, female-managed funds perform better on both the upside and the downside than do male-managed funds. But there's more to discover yet about the temperament and tendencies of women in the world of investing.

A recent report out from the National Council for Research on Women,[11] imploring the financial industry to add more women to fund-management positions, highlighted many of the studies and surveys about women and investing. Of course, the council has a strong point of view, and the report seeks to persuade the industry that adding more women will result in better investment returns, less risk taking, and the benefits that come from having diversity of thought. Looking at what we've already learned, seems they've got a point.

What's interesting here, though, are two specific findings highlighted in the report: Women research their investment decisions more thoroughly than men do, and second, they are less likely to bend to peer pressure.

The report points to a 2002 study in the *International Journal of Bank Marketing* that showed that women dig deeper, analyze more information and details, and are more likely to consider all information relating to a possible investment, even if it contradicts their initial research. In short, they want to know as much as they can and they take the time to learn it. Men, on the other hand, tend to take shortcuts with information, looking at the broadest factors and skipping data that goes against their initial thoughts. In other words, men keep it simple and move ahead; women like to get into the nitty-gritty and take their time. This makes sense when we consider the differing attitudes toward risk we've already discussed.

The next finding is even more fascinating. A 2008 University of California, Santa Barbara, study found that when men are being observed and judged by other men they consider of equal status (or, their peers), they tend to make riskier decisions than necessary in times of strife or loss, in an attempt to assert dominance. Worse still, even when the outcome would have been exactly the same had less risk been taken, the guys *still* chose the riskier path.

Women didn't have this same reaction; they chose the same path regardless of who was observing them. They seem better able to avoid posturing and make decisions based on the factors at hand, versus trying to one-up a perceived competitor. Thinking about this peer pressure effect in the context of the financial crisis, where trading floors and boardrooms were filled with men trying to outdo one another, is fascinating, and also troubling. It just goes to show that peer pressure isn't just an issue for thirteen-year-old girls battling it out on the mean streets of the suburban junior high school ("Seriously? She said *what* about me?").

■ YOU MUST BE MISTAKEN

Helping characterize our female investor, whom we've already discovered tends to trade less, take less risk, be more realistic, withstand the temptation of panicked moves in moments of market mayhem, conduct more thorough research, and resist peer pressure, is this bit of data about learning from mistakes. Merrill Lynch Investment Managers, now a part of BlackRock, conducted a nationwide telephone poll in 2004 of a thousand investors (500 men and 500 women).[12] Yet again, some key differences in temperament between female investors and male investors cropped up.

The Merrill survey found that men were more likely to buy a "hot investment without doing any research" (24 percent versus 13 percent). Of the men who admitted to this mistake, 63 percent copped to doing it more than once. Forty-seven percent of women who committed the same error did it again. We shouldn't be surprised to learn that men, when asked in the survey about which emotions played a part in their investment errors, cited greed, overconfidence, and impatience much more than women did.

Recognizing that you've made a mistake and then taking the steps to learn from it so that you don't repeat it is important for investors. As we'll see later, Warren Buffett is especially good at this. And at least based on this survey, and given what we've learned so far about overconfidence and the effect it can have on clear thinking, it appears that women have the edge here, too.

■ **BLAME IT ON THE HORMONES**

Behavioral economics has shown us that women are more risk averse than men, that they trade less and their portfolios perform better, that they are more realistic, that they are more consistent investors, and that they tend to engage in more thorough research and ignore peer pressure. Thanks to years of work in behavioral economics and finance by people like Terrance Odean and Brad Barber, we have a good grasp of what makes female investors' temperaments, on the whole, more desirable.

Recent studies from the emerging field of neuroeconomics show us something else entirely: Women's relative lack of testosterone compared to men means they may actually be hardwired to be calmer, more disciplined investors. (Sorry, guys.) Neuroeconomics (the term was reportedly coined by Professor Paul Zak of Claremont Graduate University) seeks to combine "methods from neuroscience and economics to study how people make decisions involving risk, as well as strategic decisions involving relationships with others."[13] By looking at the way chemicals within the body affect our brains and thinking patterns, this exciting area of study opens up a world of new possibilities for understanding financial decision making and risk taking.

John M. Coates, of the University of Cambridge, shook the world of finance in 2008 when he released the preliminary results of a study he did involving testosterone, cortisol, and trading profits.[14] Coates, along with coauthor Joe Herbert, gathered saliva samples from seventeen traders in London twice a day for eight days, and tracked the traders' testosterone and cortisol levels. Coates then followed up his earlier study by coauthoring another, more detailed study, based on the findings involving those seventeen traders and their testosterone and cortisol levels.[15] That's the study we'll dig into here. (Don't be afraid—science can be fun, I promise.)

These traders were involved with highly active speculation, holding mostly futures contract positions (a complex form of financial instrument that involves betting on the future price of a commodity or stock index), in some cases for mere seconds. We aren't talking about your typical individual stock investors here, but nonetheless, the findings are fascinating and have potentially broad implications.

(In case you need a high school biology refresher, testosterone and cortisol are both natural steroids [a type of hormone] that help our minds and bodies in instinctual situations such as fight or flight, and propel us to mate as well as strive for success and status.)

Relying on two prior theories about testosterone, the "challenge" hypothesis and the "winner effect," the scientists set out to measure how testosterone affects financial risk taking. The "challenge" hypothesis suggests that in males, testosterone levels initially rise just as high as are needed for sexual activity; they rise higher only when the male is confronted with a threat, creating aggression.

However, the "challenge" hypothesis has been easier to find evidence for in animal studies than in human studies, owing in part to the fact that our highly developed brains can overcome more of the effects of hormones than other species can. Further, it's hard to pin down exactly what each study means and how each study measures rather nebulous topics like "aggression." This is one reason the British scientists were optimistic about their study—it's easy to quantify and measure a trader's profits and losses, for instance. Not much wiggle room there. Also, while male traders may not become "aggressive" to the point of picking fights and getting physical, a "challenge" still exists for them in the form of competition with one another for ever higher returns. (Remember, too, what we learned earlier about the effects of peer pressure on men.)

The "winner effect," on the other hand, is well documented in both the animal kingdom and in the world of sports.

Basically, it describes the way testosterone levels work in competitors, either in a battle between animals, or a battle between athletes or sports teams. Put simply, testosterone levels rise in anticipation of a confrontation or competition. The winning animal or athlete, however, comes out on the other side with higher testosterone levels, and the loser with, well, you guessed it—lower testosterone levels (and undoubtedly his tail, figuratively or otherwise, between his legs). What's even more intriguing is that winning leads to higher testosterone, which leads to more winning, which creates a feedback loop of victory and heightened testosterone levels. Hence the "winner effect."

So by framing their research with the "challenge" hypothesis and the "winner effect," the authors wanted to see if there was a correlation between testosterone levels and the traders' most profitable days. They discovered that on days when the traders were the most successful, and made the most money, they indeed exhibited the highest levels of testosterone.

Visions of bulging neck veins, red faces, and sweating, screaming traders aside, this research suggests that higher levels of testosterone may have helped these traders better sort through lots of information in a quicker period of time. It also likely helped them make fast, risky decisions. The style of "high-frequency" trading these guys were engaging in was the perfect expression of testosterone's benefits. The authors shared a belief that for other, more measured styles of investing, testosterone's benefits may actually hurt results. They also noted that this kind of frenetic trading actually has a physical component to it as well, which may also have benefited from the presence of increased levels of testosterone.

The other hormone in play here, cortisol, rises in stressful situations. Thus the scientists believed it would jump when traders started losing money. However, that's not what they found, exactly. Cortisol levels did rise, but it wasn't related to traders losing money. Instead, rises in cortisol showed a correlation with rises in market volatility.

Cortisol helps us prepare for the unexpected and the uncertain, and market volatility creates scenarios that are highly uncertain. Quoting from the study, "Our results raise the possibility that while testosterone codes for economic return, cortisol codes for risk." [16] So when markets are going haywire, and traders aren't sure what's coming next, their cortisol levels jump, prepping them to be ready for the unknown.

All right, so if we know that highly successful traders have increased levels of testosterone, and we know that their bodies respond to market volatility and uncertainty by producing more of the stress hormone cortisol, what's it all mean for both female and male investors and the financial markets at large? Well, it's the flip side of these positive effects of testosterone and cortisol that can harm individual results, and possibly, when looked at from a macro perspective, even harm our financial markets.

Taking a look at cortisol first, the study finds that when cortisol reaches certain levels, it can actually start hurting performance by making traders irrationally risk *averse*. They see danger behind every market movement, boogeymen behind every ticker symbol or flicker on the screen. When cortisol levels are too elevated for too long, and the condition becomes chronic, it can become a nearly self-fulfilling prophecy, with traders unwilling to act even when it's the smart thing to do, and even when it's in their best interest to do so. Fear settles in, anxiety takes hold, and cortisol's grip is secure.

At a macro level, this mental paralysis can possibly result in a market downturn becoming more protracted than it otherwise would be. Volatility begets cortisol which begets fear which begets even more volatility and on and on. It can potentially add to an already plummeting market, making a scary drop even worse.

Testosterone, as we mentioned earlier, can help traders take risks and move fast, making loads of money in the meantime. But too much testosterone for too long can encourage too much risk taking, and the profitable testosterone-laden trader of today can end up reversing course tomorrow. Throw in some market volatility and we find that a blazing risk taker can quickly become nervous about risk, effectively throwing the market on its head. The study's conclusion, then, is not necessarily that market bubbles and crashes are caused by hormones, but they do suggest that "hormones may exaggerate moves once under way."[17]

Further, the authors suggest that having more gender and age diversity in the financial markets could greatly help market stability. They point out that women have only 5–10 percent of the testosterone levels that men do, and, as we've just learned, some studies show that they are less likely to succumb to the stress and peer pressure created by competitive situations than men. There's reason to believe, then, that adding women to trading floors, boardrooms, and other male-heavy strongholds in the financial world (which is still just about all of them) would, thanks to women's naturally occurring *lack* of testosterone, "help dampen hormonal swings in the market."[18] (Insert your own joke here.)

So would the worldwide financial panic in the fall of 2008 have happened or been as severe had more women been more involved in the world of high finance, their lack of testosterone mediating the effects of the male hormone, lessening the highs and lows, calming the tempest? Of course no one can say with 100 percent certainty, but all indications point to a greater diversity of not only gender, but of thought, experience, and worldview, potentially leading to a different outcome.

■ PORTRAIT OF A FEMALE INVESTOR

The hardworking scientists and academics in the worlds of behavioral finance and neuroeconomics will undoubtedly continue to study the differences in investment behavior, attitudes, and outcomes between men and women. It's never dull, sometimes controversial, and always enlightening. Putting together what we've learned here paints a picture of what a successful investment temperament looks like, and it's awfully familiar. But before getting into the traits female investors share with Warren Buffett, what makes him the greatest investor of all time, and what we could all learn from his temperament, let's recap.

Female investors tend to:

1. Trade less than men do
2. Exhibit less overconfidence: men think they know more than they do, while women are more likely to know what they don't know
3. Shun risk more than male investors do
4. Be less optimistic, and therefore more realistic, than their male counterparts
5. Put in more time and effort researching possible investments, considering every angle and detail, as well as considering alternate points of view

6. Be more immune to peer pressure and tend to make decisions the same way regardless of who's watching
7. Learn from their mistakes
8. Have less testosterone than men do, making them less willing to take extreme risks, which, in turn, could lead to less extreme market cycles

As a result of their different approach to investing, and their temperaments, female investors also produce results that are more consistent and persistent. You can count on 'em. And in the hedge fund world, female-managed hedge funds outperform comparable male-managed hedge funds, and their results don't suffer from market drops as severely.

The above eight traits represent an investing mindset that all investors—men and women alike—should adopt. And we all can—it's possible. It won't be easy, it'll take practice and hard work, and we'll slip up from time to time, but it's possible. We're more likely to reach the same superior outcomes as female investors—and Warren Buffett, as we'll see—if we do so.

It's also important that we try. We need to bury the old Wall Street attitude of yore. As we've seen with the financial crisis, eventually it all catches up to those involved and even those who aren't. Just about everyone ends up the poorer for it. So read on as we uncover how the greatest investor of all time is actually more in tune with his feminine side than you might have realized, and why, when it comes to investing, this is a very good thing.

3

A Quick Intro to the Oracle

Before we dive into the defining characteristics of Warren Buffett's "feminine" temperament as an investor, let's learn a little background on the man whom many dub the "Oracle of Omaha."

Warren Edward Buffett was born August 30, 1930, in his beloved, bucolic Omaha, Nebraska. Not surprisingly, given all that we know about the man he was to become, he was a precocious child, showing an early interest in and aptitude for numbers, details, and moneymaking. Buffett was clearly bright and driven, and made his first foray into the world of commerce at age six, selling packs of gum.[1] He went on to make money all kinds of ways as a child, from selling Cokes at a markup around the neighborhood, to selling used golf balls to golfers at a local golf course.

When Buffett was twelve, his father was elected to Congress, forcing the family to move from Omaha to Washington, D.C. Buffett wasn't thrilled with the move, and had trouble making friends and fitting in at his new school. His love for business and hard work was rewarded, though, when he started his beloved paper route delivering the *Washington Post*.

Through this early exposure to the newspaper business, Buffett developed a love affair with the printed word that remains strong to this day.

In high school, Buffett continued his paper route success, and started additional businesses thanks to the money he made delivering all that news to all those Washingtonians. He actually bought a forty-acre farm in Nebraska, about an hour away from Omaha, and let a farmer work the land, splitting the profits with him.[2] (Remember, this is a high school student we are talking about! Remember what you were doing in high school? I bet it wasn't buying farms in Nebraska.)

Buffett first learned about stocks and investing from his father, who was a stockbroker in Omaha before becoming a congressman. He bought his first stock at age eleven, investing in Cities Service Preferred. He bought three shares for himself and three for his sister Doris, at $38 a share. Unfortunately, a short while later, the stock tanked, dropping 29 percent to $27 a share. Buffett held, but the eleven-year-old was bothered by the fact that he'd lost his sister money. He hated losing money himself, of course, but knowing that he'd dragged his sister along for the depressing ride troubled him. When Cities Service rose again, to $40, Buffett sold, taking a $5 profit for them both combined. Then, naturally, Cities Service skyrocketed to $200 a share.[3] For the young eventual guru, this incident, and his apparent lack of patience, wasn't something he'd soon forget.

THE EARLY BIRD GETS THE RETURN

Think Buffett started investing young? Well, value investor and owner of Lauren Templeton Capital Management, Lauren Templeton (great-niece of renowned international value investor Sir John Templeton), started even younger. She said in a September 2010 interview:

"[B]ecause I grew up in the Templeton family we are really a family of value investors. I started buying stocks when I was seven or eight years old. My dad would allow me to buy one share a month of any stock I wanted. He would buy it for me. And then he would take the stock certificate, because at the time they mailed you an actual certificate, and he would mat and frame the stock certificate and hang it on the walls of my room. So when I was a child, my room was literally wallpapered with stock certificates.

"At first, like any child would, I bought very familiar companies—like Disney, Wal-Mart, the Gap . . . It was very important to have these stock certificates hanging on the walls of my room because all of a sudden, I really did, as a child, think of myself as an owner of one of these companies. I can remember telling friends on the playground that, yes, I did own part of Disney. And they couldn't believe it."[4]

Now, I'm not suggesting you're sunk if you didn't start investing at eleven as Buffett did, or eight as Lauren Templeton did, but starting as early as possible is a key to investing success. You may have missed the preteen investing boat yourself, but surely you know children who haven't, be it a son or daughter, a niece or nephew, or the young progeny of a friend. Without a doubt it's a challenge to get children interested in investing, especially given the ridiculous number of distractions in the world today, but it's worth a try.

Make it fun by pointing out the products of companies you've bought shares of at the grocery store or shopping mall. Motley Fool cofounders and brothers David and Tom Gardner talk about seeing chocolate pudding at the grocery store with their father as kids and being told that they owned the company that made it, a statement that made quite an impression on them. Believe it or not, tying the esoteric idea of "investing" to something tangible like chocolate pud-

After finishing his undergraduate degree at the University of Nebraska, Buffett set his eyes on business school at Harvard. However, fate intervened, and Buffett was rejected from Harvard (in a decision sort of like Decca Records rejecting the Beatles in 1961) and ended up at Columbia Business School. There he would meet the man who would become his biggest influence and mentor, the master of value investing himself, Benjamin Graham, who at that time was a professor at Columbia. David Dodd, who co-wrote *the* textbook on investing, *Security Analysis*, with Graham, was the head of Columbia's department of finance and a professor. So here were both Graham and Dodd, in one spot, at one school. This was the place for Buffett to become *Buffett*.

Buffett had recently read Graham's second book, *The Intelligent Investor*, and in it he found his calling as an investor—he was to be a "value" guy. And he was about to learn from Graham himself, an experience that can't be underestimated for Buffett and his future. Had Harvard said yes, the world still would have been blessed with a quirky intellectual numbers guy, running myriad businesses, undoubtedly interested in stocks, perhaps still becoming a value investing disciple. But thanks to his own temperament, his experience at Columbia, and Graham's direct influence on him, we were instead given the greatest investor of all time.

Upon graduating from Columbia, Buffett, who had soaked up every bit of Graham and Dodd he possibly could, wanted even more, and that meant working for Graham's investment firm, Graham-Newman Corporation. He interviewed with Graham and was turned down cold. At that time, the big Wall Street investment houses discriminated against Jews, and Graham liked to keep the few spots available at his firm open for them. Buffett was sent packing, back to Omaha.

Once home, he got a job at his father's brokerage house, where he, like every other stockbroker working there and elsewhere, called people up and tried to convince them to buy shares of certain companies. The job was more about marketing than actual research and analysis. Buffett was successful with the people he knew; after all, his family and friends knew how smart he was and trusted him. But outside that group, he struggled.[5]

Buffett stayed in contact with Graham, and a few years later was indeed given his shot to work for his mentor. He left Omaha once again, moved to New York City, and went to work at Graham-Newman, analyzing companies and suggesting undervalued ones for the firm to invest in. He was much happier as an analyst than he had been as, essentially, a salesman at his father's brokerage. This played to Buffett's strengths and studious nature, allowing him to shine.

Buffett's Graham-Newman heyday didn't last long, though. In 1956, after Buffett had been there only about two years, Graham decided to leave his firm and retire. That was it for Buffett as well. Despite being offered the opportunity to become a partner in the firm, Buffett struck out on his own. He started Buffett Associates, Ltd., an investment partnership similar to the one Graham had operated. In the beginning, the partnership had just seven partners, a mix of family, friends, and Buffett himself. The initial stakes were $100 from Buffett and $105,000 from the other six partners.

After helping Graham shut down his firm in New York, Buffett returned to Omaha for good, where he could create the life he wanted, working from home, spending all his time reading and researching investments. Graham himself suggested to some of his former clients that they invest money with the young upstart in Nebraska, the one no one'd ever heard of. But that anonymity wouldn't last long. With outsized returns, and a fee structure that rewarded Buffett only when he made his partners money, it was just a matter of time before word got around that something special was happening in Omaha (of all places).

And special it was. At the time of the partnership's closing in 1969, Buffett's partners had earned a 32 percent average annual return before fees. That's simply unheard-of; it was then and remains so today.

In 1962, Buffett began buying shares for the partnership of a small New England textile maker, Berkshire Hathaway, which he believed was undervalued. Buffett hoped that the company's then president would buy back his shares; he'd never intended to keep the company for good. After all, the textile industry was in decline, and Berkshire had put up nine years of losses. Buffett believed he could buy shares on the cheap and then sell them back to the company at a higher price.

However, Berkshire's president had a different idea, and after a somewhat nasty affair wherein Buffett believed he'd been promised one price for his shares and then offered another, he (Buffett) decided he in fact wanted all of Berkshire

Hathaway. And though he would later come to regret it, calling it "the dumbest stock I ever bought" and estimating that it cost him $200 billion in opportunity cost, he eventually got it.[6]

After trying unsuccessfully to make the company competitive and profitable, Buffett shut down Berkshire Hathaway's textile business in 1985. But he kept the actual company, transforming it into the investment powerhouse we associate with him today. Along with his longtime friend and business partner, Charlie Munger, Buffett has been able to turn Berkshire Hathaway into what is known as a holding company—that is, it owns whole businesses or parts of businesses in an array of industries, everything from Coca-Cola to GEICO Insurance to See's Candies to Dairy Queen to the Washington Post Company.

But the real original genius of Berkshire Hathaway can be found in the concept known as "float," a by-product of the insurance business. Put simply, when you pay an insurance company a premium for your car or home (for instance), the company gets to keep that money from you—and from the millions of other policyholders who use its services—until it has to pay out for claims. That money is available for investment, and Buffett exploits this source of excess cash like no other, using it to tack on additional businesses, buy stock in other companies, and generally let the power of compound interest work to his, and his shareholders', advantage.

It's worked beautifully. From 1965 to 2010, Berkshire Hathaway's compounded annual gain in per-share book value has been a remarkable 20.2 percent versus the S&P 500's paltry-by-comparison 9.4 percent total return, including dividends. (The returns for Berkshire are actually understated, because Buffett insists on reporting them in Berkshire's annual reports as after-tax, while the S&P returns are given as pretax figures.)

Now that we have a little background on Buffett, let's get into what created those results, and what makes his investing style and philosophy so, well, *girly*. But first, because it'll come in handy to keep these in mind as we go forward, a quick refresher on the feminine investing traits we learned about earlier:

Female investors tend to:

1. Trade less than men do
2. Exhibit less overconfidence: men think they know more than they do, while women are more likely to know what they don't know
3. Shun risk more than male investors do
4. Be less optimistic, and therefore more realistic, than their male counterparts
5. Put in more time and effort researching possible investments, considering every angle and detail, as well as considering alternate points of view
6. Be more immune to peer pressure and tend to make decisions the same way regardless of who's watching
7. Learn from their mistakes
8. Have less testosterone than men do, making them less willing to take extreme risks, which, in turn, could lead to less extreme market cycles

Thanks to these eight traits, as we saw in chapter 2, women produce results that are more consistent and persistent.

As we'll see, Buffett manages to provide us with examples of all these traits, and with a track record like his, it would be silly for all of us not to get a little girly right alongside him.

(If you now have an image in your head of Warren Buffett putting on lipstick and carrying a purse, I'm sorry.)

4

Trade Less, Make More

Famous for saying that his "favorite holding period is forever," Buffett really is the king of the "trade less," buy-and-hold school of thought.[1] In fact, he is so vehemently opposed to short-term trading that he once advocated (perhaps sarcastically) for a drastic change in tax policy—one that would tax profits gained from short-term trades (defined as any holding bought and sold under a year) at 100 *percent*.[2] Regardless of his seriousness about the 100 percent tax, Buffett did sign an Aspen Institute petition in September 2009 calling for the tax code to reward long-term investment versus short-term speculation.[3] This is an issue that Buffett's been passionate about for years.

Holding on to the companies you invest in is important to Buffett because he likes to emphasize that when you buy a stock, you aren't just buying a three-or-four-letter ticker, dancing across the screen like some mythical secret code. No, you're buying a piece of a living, breathing company. Understanding this—that you are buying into an actual business—is an investing truth Buffett learned and took to heart from his mentor Ben Graham.

There's no difference in Buffett's eyes, nor should there be in yours, between investing in a publicly traded company and buying outright, for example, the sandwich shop down the street. They each represent ownership of a business; the difference just comes down to how much you own—the whole thing, or a part. (Although perhaps as the owner of the sandwich shop, you'd get a discount on that delicious turkey sub you like so much—shareholders aren't guaranteed such special treatment. On the other hand, that sandwich shop probably won't pay you a dividend, which a lot of public companies will. Everything's a trade-off, isn't it?)

Owning stock in a company represents an important decision, and one that shouldn't be taken lightly. The image we have in our heads of Wall Street traders, yelling and frantically making buys and sells, flipping in and out of one stock after another, is precisely the opposite of the man Warren Buffett is—calculated, thoughtful, measured, and patient. It's possible that some of those traders couldn't even tell you anything about the companies they just churned into and out of, besides their ticker symbols. They probably couldn't tell you what industry the company's in, what good or service it sells, how long it's been around, or who its executives are.

Buffett, on the other hand, first discovered his fondness for insurance company GEICO when he was in graduate school at Columbia. He bought shares then, and would eventually buy the whole company for Berkshire Hathaway. Since he was a boy throwing papers in the misty early morning hours in D.C., he's loved newspapers and the *Washington Post* (which he's been a large shareholder of since the 1970s). He's owned his shares of soft drink giant Coca-Cola since the late 1980s.

Buffett understands that he is an owner of an actual business, and affords this the gravity it deserves.

Buffett's feelings on this extend to Berkshire Hathaway and its shareholders, too. In Buffett's so-called "Owner's Manual," which he wrote to illustrate his and Charlie Munger's philosophies for their shareholders, the very first principle preaches the importance of realizing that you are a "part owner" of an actual business. As such, they hope that Berkshire shareholders won't sell their stock, just as Berkshire wouldn't abandon longtime holdings Coca-Cola and American Express, two examples Buffett gives. Quoting from the Manual, "In fact, we would not care in the least if several years went by in which there was no trading, or quotation of prices, in the stocks of those companies."[4]

Berkshire shareholders appear to have gotten Buffett's message. The turnover in shares of Berkshire is remarkably low, with some shareholders even willing their shares to future generations in an effort to keep their heirs from selling after they're gone. From the grave, even, it seems Buffett's advice resonates.

Buffett also likes to encourage investors to think of their investment decisions as represented by a punchcard containing "just twenty punches" meant to last a lifetime. "With every investment decision his card is punched, and he has one fewer available for the rest of his life."[5] Buffett adds, "You'll never use up all 20 punches if you save them for great ideas."[6]

Thinking of your investment decisions this way is helpful, although it can be a bit unrealistic. Investors without Buffett's seemingly unlimited amount of cash may have to decide to sell certain companies in order to buy others—decisions Buffett himself was faced with early on in his investing career, and, indeed, continues to encounter when making large acquisitions. There's no shame in that. However, think seriously about investing your money in a company. What you are essentially saying when you push that little "buy" button on your online brokerage account screen is that the company you are investing in is *the best place* at that precise moment for your money—otherwise, you'd invest the money elsewhere, right? As Buffett has said, "If you aren't willing to own a stock for ten years, don't even think about owning it for ten minutes."[7]

In an email interview, Prem Jain, professor at the Georgetown University McDonough School of Business and author of *Buffett Beyond Value: Why Buffett Looks to Growth and Management When Investing*, said of Buffett's unique point of view, "Warren Buffett's most important quality, I believe, is his focus on the long term. He does not pay much attention to what the so-called experts are predicting about the next year or two. Most people in the market are seeking short-term returns. When there is some bad news, far too many people react negatively and the stock market goes down. Similarly, people become euphoric en masse from time to time, which often produces bubbles. Buffett's levelheaded temperament allows him to weather these fluctuations.

"Having a long-term view becomes a tremendous advantage in a world where most others are short-term oriented. When the herd of short-term investors moves the market, the independent-minded long-term investors can take the opposite side and eventually earn superior returns."[8]

Buffett's patience is another important characteristic that defines his investing style and temperament. He's willing to wait, sitting atop piles of cash, until he finds the perfect opportunity to invest. This can mean enduring frustrating periods of watching the market scream to ever new heights, while you sit on the proverbial sidelines, waiting for good companies to become more fairly valued, and watching your pile of cash struggle to keep up with inflation.

But you've got to have the fortitude to do it. Buffett has slipped (hey, he *is* human) a couple of times in his history, investing in companies that weren't up to his usual standards because the pickings were otherwise slim, and each time he came to regret it. US Airways, which Berkshire invested in in 1989, is one notable and notorious example of this. (We'll talk more about Buffett's US Airways debacle in the chapter on mistakes.)

We're all in danger of making mistakes like this, but if you do, just learn from it as Buffett did and move on. Instead of beating yourself up, you've got to focus on learning to be patient, to stay put, and to wait until the market makes it worth your while to invest your hard-earned cash in a company. As Buffett said at Berkshire's annual meeting in 1998 (a time when he was being criticized for not participating in the market's rise), "We're not going to buy anything just to buy it. We will only buy something if we think we're getting something attractive. . . . You don't get paid for activity. You get paid for being right."[9]

Buffett likes to talk about waiting for the "fat pitch" to come and the freedom that gives investors to avoid mistakes. In an interview with the *New York Times* in 2007, he explained his thinking this way: "What's nice about investing is you don't have to swing at pitches. You can watch pitches come in one inch above or once inch below your navel, and you don't have to swing. No umpire is going to call you out. You can wait for the pitch you want."[10]

Luckily for us, unlike baseball players under pressure from coaches and their fans to swing, we have the luxury of waiting without anyone getting impatient but ourselves—and that impatience is something we can learn to tackle. It can be tempting to jump in when you see stocks rise (and that's made all the worse by listening to financial media hoopla and nonsense), but don't. Exercise restraint. Your portfolio will be the richer for it.

RESISTING THE URGE TO "DO SOMETHING"

Value investor Lisa Rapuano, founder of Lane Five Capital Management, also believes in and employs this long-term mindset in her business. As she said in a September 2010 interview, "I am very good at ignoring noise, the day-to-day stuff just isn't important, and I will go months without trading. I'm not sure how people who trade every day and are looking at short-term trends and optimizing trading strategies and things like that sleep at night. For me, it's patience, it's low activity, it's thoughtful, it's moving more deliberately. I don't know why I have been particularly good at doing that, but I do know that it's an advantage that I have over a lot of people. I just don't feel the need to 'do something' a lot of times."[11]

Buffett himself was patient during the last several years, letting around $44 billion in cash (yes, that's with a *b*) sit on Berkshire's balance sheet during 2004, 2005, 2006, and 2007.[12] Buffett waited and waited for his fat pitch and finally found it when the market dropped in the fall of 2008 amid the financial crisis. He jumped in, spending $20 billion snatching up pieces of General Electric and Goldman Sachs, and encouraging others to stare down panic and fear and take advantage of the great opportunities the market was presenting them at that time. As he's often quoted as saying, in one of his most famous and enduring (and endearing) turns of phrase, "Be greedy when others are fearful, and fearful when others are greedy."

Patience is also important once you've made the leap and actually invested in a company. Sometimes things go wrong and just after you've purchased your stock, it falls. It's inevitable that this will happen to every investor at least once, immediately making you doubt your decision-making process. Perhaps the market as a whole swoons, or perhaps it's just your particular investment that seems to have forgotten that you bought it so it would increase in value, not the other way around. Either way, it can be incredibly disheartening to watch what you were sure was a, well, sure thing turn out seemingly otherwise.

But you can't just panic and sell. If you do your homework and stand by your investment convictions, you've got to stick it out. You've got to be patient, and not fall into a trap of trading away any shot you've got at long-term success.

Buffett faced a similar situation when Berkshire started buying shares of the Washington Post Company in 1973. Right off the bat, in the midst of a horrible bear market second only to the one we just endured, the stock dropped 20 percent and hovered there until 1976—three whole years! It took until 1981 for the Post to reach the value Buffett believed it deserved.[13]

And now? Buffett's held on to his shares of the Post through recessions and recoveries and more than a few American presidencies and it's one of his most successful investments of all time—a true "primary" holding that Buffett intends to keep "permanently" for Berkshire.[14] Had he bolted at the first sign of market turmoil, he would have missed out on a gigantic winner. Patience can be painful, but it's worth it in the end.

Being a successful investor isn't easy. It requires fortitude, strength, preparation, and a willingness to avoid acting just for the sake of "doing something." To get there, keep the following in mind:

- Remember you're buying a piece of an actual business.
- Take the long view.
- Be patient.

5

Rein in Overconfidence

In addition to his solidly long-term philosophy, another of Buffett's most famous and defining characteristics is his insistence on staying within his circle of competence—or knowing what he knows and knowing what he doesn't know. For Buffett, it's critical that you know what it is you're investing in. You're an owner of a business, after all, and you wouldn't think of opening up a company or buying a part of one you didn't fully understand, right?

Buffett's most notorious for his avoidance of technology companies, citing them over the years as lying outside his "sphere of understanding" (despite his close friendship with Microsoft cofounder Bill Gates).[1] Though he may try to argue otherwise, it's not so much that Buffett lacks the ability or insight to understand what every technology company does, and how they make money (or don't, as the case may be). Sure, there may be the odd super technical advanced mumbo-jumbo company that would be beyond Buffett's comprehension, but that's not the real issue for him with tech.

It's more that he doesn't consider himself able to predict

the competitive landscape for technology companies. He's not able with enough certainty to make himself feel comfortable, to get a grasp on the future economics of the technology industry. He recognizes it as fast moving, ever changing, and potentially deadly to the average, or even above-average, investor. There are too many variables involved, too many unknowns, that can render a well-thought-out investment dead and gone in what seems like mere moments.

Remember hot technology companies from the late 1990s and early 2000 like WebVan, Pets.com, and Boo.com? Anyone know where they are now? The landscape for these companies changed, and changed fast. Because Buffett can't predict how the competition's going to look for a technology company fifty years from now, he won't bother. There are lots of other companies out there that he can understand fully, feeling confident in their prospects.

Two keys to understanding how Buffett invests are the related concepts of "economic moat" and "sustainable competitive advantage." Think of the idea of a moat just as you would the traditional fairy-tale moat around a castle, keeping a pretty long-haired girl protected from hungry dragons and lustful princes. A moat, in the business world, protects the company and its profit-making potential from hungry and lustful competitors. It's anything that separates a company and gives it an advantage over its competition, resulting in higher profits for longer periods of time.

A company like Coca-Cola is protected by its brand, for example, giving it a competitive advantage Buffett can understand and reliably count on in the future. It would be incredibly difficult for an upstart soda outfit to come in and compete effectively enough with Coke at this point to inflict serious injury on it. The company's moat is too wide, its reach too far, and its products enjoyed by too many people the world over. Buffett can look ahead 150 years in the future and he can imagine people teleporting all across the globe, downloading music directly into their brain, and all the while happily putting a $5 bill into a Vend-o-tron to synthesize and drink their favorite Coke product. The strength in Coke's brand and business makes it so.

It's vital, too, that the competitive advantages be "durable" or "sustainable." Quoting Buffett himself talking in 1999 about the state of the stock market and the insane prices for technology companies (which he compared to other revolutionary yet ultimately money-losing societal advances like autos and airplanes), "The key to investing is not assessing how much an industry is going to affect society, or how much it will grow, but rather determining the competitive advantage of any given company and, above all, the durability of that advantage. The products or services that have wide, sustainable moats around them are the ones that deliver rewards to investors."[2]

This is what is lacking in the world of technology for Buffett. He can't see the moats, and he can't predict just which companies are going to survive, much less thrive. In other words, he knows what he knows, and what he doesn't know, and he sticks to it.

Buffett's aversion to investing in technology didn't just happen in the 1980s or 1990s, though. He passed on a chance to invest in computer processing giant Intel in the 1960s, then just a wee start-up, even though he knew and trusted one of its founders.[3] He simply couldn't be sure he understood the company and its prospects well enough to put his money behind it. (It was a costly choice, but his conviction to stay within his circle of competence is admirable, nonetheless.)

And in a letter to his partners in 1967, when the market around him was jumping with popular new technology investments, leaving Buffett looking for ideas he felt comfortable investing in, he stayed true to himself, saying, "We will not go into businesses where technology which is way over my head is crucial to the investment decision. I know about as much about semi-conductors or integrated circuits as I do of the mating habits of the chrzaszcz."[4]

The lesson for investors here isn't necessarily that we should avoid technology just because Buffett does, but rather that we should understand and abide by our own circles of competence. Maybe you work in the world of high-tech, and are therefore uniquely positioned to have insights into the flashy companies Buffett wouldn't even entertain investing in. Or perhaps you're in the health-care industry, another area that can be complicated and difficult to understand, and you can rattle off the names and competitive advantages of pharmaceutical stocks galore. If so, excellent—don't be afraid to use that knowledge. If not, though, don't worry about sticking to your knitting, things you know and understand. Buffett proves you can make a *pretty* good living investing in less complex companies.

UNDERSTANDING THE KEY TO VALUATION

In an interview conducted in September 2010, value investor Lauren Templeton agreed that staying within your circle of competence is the smart strategy. She said, "As a value investor, if I can't value it, I can't invest in it. So that kept us out of a lot of financial stocks that were showing up in our screens during the financial crisis. We couldn't get our arms around the balance sheets so we couldn't invest in them. How do you value something if you really don't have a transparent view of the balance sheet? Of course that keeps us out of biotech and industries like that where there's just no good way for us to value the company. So if we can't value it, we can't invest in it."[5]

As long as he's been investing (and that's been quite a while—he bought his first stock when he was eleven, remember?), Buffett's focused on companies and industries he understands. In fact, things he loved as a child sometimes show up among his investment ideas later, meaning that in some cases he established his circle of competence quite early in his life. He even said in his 1982 shareholder letter, tongue no doubt in cheek, "nostalgia should be weighted heavily in stock selection," citing GEICO and the Washington Post Company.[6]

Speaking of the Post, as mentioned earlier, he developed a love for newspapers in general, and the *Washington Post* in particular, early in his life. After exercising his arm hurling all those newspapers onto porches so long ago, he now owns about 20 percent of the Washington Post Company, which he started buying way back in the 1970s. He's also owned other newspapers over the years, including the now-defunct *Omaha Sun* and the still-going *Buffalo News*.

Take railroads, too. Buffett has long been fascinated with railroads, and had a small electric train set when he was a boy. He expanded it to a larger one in his attic later on and loved showing it off to friends and colleagues. In 2007, Berkshire began buying shares of freight rail company Burlington

Northern Santa Fe, and in 2009 made a successful bid to buy the company outright. Now Buffett can benefit from what he sees as an energy-efficient, low-cost way to ship goods in the United States and can own a railroad that's way beyond just a toy train. (Ah, every little budding capitalist's dream.)

Many of Buffett's, and Berkshire's, investments over the years have been consumer brands that are easy to follow, easy to understand, and easy to imagine enthusiastically owning a piece of. In some cases, Berkshire owns the entire company outright; in others it owns shares just like any other investor (although naturally it owns much, much more).

Berkshire owns Dairy Queen, See's Candies, and Fruit of the Loom outright, for example. So we're looking at burgers and Blizzards, chocolate and undies—all easy to grasp. Berkshire also owns the Nebraska Furniture Mart and Borsheim's Fine Jewelry, adding a giant furniture retailer and a fancy baubles shop to the list. And as we mentioned earlier, Berkshire owns a chunk of Coca-Cola, and at one time or another has owned shares of Nike, Costco, Wal-Mart, Kraft Foods, and Procter & Gamble (maker of Crest toothpaste, Gillette razors, Bounty paper towels, Duracell batteries, and Tide detergent, just to name a few). These are big, recognizable companies, producing goods and providing services most of us have used or at least encountered in our lifetime.

All these businesses are signature Buffett. They have wide moats and strong competitive advantages, making it easy for Buffett to analyze them and predict their futures. They're easy to understand and get your head around. And, while less tangible, it has to be said that they're fun to own and follow. Who doesn't like seeing Oreos at the grocery store, for instance, and thinking, "Hey, I own shares of Kraft—therefore I own the company making those cookies!" It makes investing relatable when you can look around and see the evidence of your money at work. Buffett enjoys this aspect of investing, as well. (On the flip side, it's just not as jazzy to say, "Hey, I own the company that applies the coating of the oxide layers onto the aluminum electrolytic capacitors of this very computer's motherboard!")

Buffett's circle of competence also includes insurance and financial companies. GEICO, the insurance company perhaps best known for its clever commercials (do you prefer the cavemen or the gecko?), is a significant part of Berkshire Hathaway, as are other, smaller insurance companies. As we talked about earlier, they provide Buffett with "float" or excess cash that he can put to work investing. Berkshire's also owned shares of American Express for years, and has invested in banks like Wells Fargo, U.S. Bancorp, and Goldman Sachs as well.

Maybe your own circle of competence doesn't include banks and insurance companies. That's no problem. The key lesson here is to recognize what you do know and understand, and to leave the rest alone. Be honest with yourself and remember the perils of overconfidence. Another point to remember is that just investing within your circle of competence without doing any further research isn't enough. You still have to do your homework on the companies to be sure they'll make good investments for the long term. Basing an investment decision only on knowing that you love Starbucks lattes won't fly, for instance, but it's a good starting point for your research.

Investing in companies you understand is important, so remember:

- Buffett's "sphere of understanding" may be different from your own.
- Think about and learn what your own circle of competence covers.
- Stick to it, no matter what.

6

Shun Risk

Buffett believes that long-term-focused investing within your circle of competence will result in wealth for smart investors. This view is complemented by his risk-averse nature. All investing involves risk, naturally. There are unknowns inherent in making the choice to trade your money for a piece of a company—the future is never certain, after all. But Buffett believes that to be as successful as possible, you should do everything you can to limit your risk, and therefore lessen the likelihood that you'll lose all-important capital (or money you can invest). He believes in tilting the scales as far as possible away from speculation and toward an ownership-minded investing framework.

We've already learned about moats and competitive advantages, so now's the time to embrace the concept that Buffett has called "the cornerstone of investment success."[1] That important concept is called "margin of safety."

Like much of his investing philosophy, Buffett learned about the idea of margin of safety from Ben Graham. This principle was key to Graham's value investing school of thought, and the concept even gets its very own chapter in *The Intelligent*

Investor. Without getting too much into financial nitty-gritty here, a margin of safety represents the leeway investors give themselves when purchasing shares of a company. Graham believed that because investors can't with precise certainty know how much a company is actually worth (a best estimate is still just that—an estimate), you should reduce your risk of both being wrong and of being subjected to the market's vagaries by giving yourself an appropriate margin of safety.

For example, let's say you believe ABC company is worth $100 a share, and it's currently trading at $75 a pop. Buying shares at that price would give you a margin of safety of 25 percent (some value investors insist on at least a 40–50 percent margin of safety). Instituting a margin of safety for your stock purchases is a way of managing the risk involved with investing, and the wider the margin, the more protection you give yourself. You can even adjust your required margin of safety to be higher with certain industries, such as more volatile or unpredictable ones, and lower with bigger, more established and reliable companies. The goal is to limit your losses, not eliminate the possibility of them altogether—that would be ideal, of course, yet impossible.

For Buffett, the concept of margin of safety is integral to the act of investing as a way to manage risk. He's often quoted as saying, "Rule No. 1: Never lose money. Rule No. 2: Never forget Rule No. 1."[2] It's unfortunately a certainty that every investor is going to lose *some* money at some point, but Buffett's point here is to focus on doing what you can to avoid losing more than you have to. Sounds easy, yes, but the truth is that making hasty decisions and paying more for a company than you should can saddle your portfolio with losses that can take years to undo, as well as shrink your precious capital. Preserving the capital you have to invest is of paramount importance, and you should do everything you can to guard against the loss of this capital. Buying with a margin of safety in place helps lessen this possibility.

Back in the 1970s, as we mentioned before, Berkshire started buying shares of the Washington Post Company. After analyzing it, Buffett believed its assets were worth at least $400 million, yet the market was giving it a price tag of less than $100 million.[3] This represented a margin of safety of 75 percent—a steal! Berkshire bought shares and held on, though Buffett wasn't initially rewarded for his prescience. As we also discussed earlier, right after Buffett invested in the Post, shares dropped and remained below what Buffett thought they were worth for three years.

This illustrates another important point about margin of safety—Buffett had done his homework and was certain the market was mispricing the Post, woefully so, in fact. He could be comfortable being patient and holding on to his shares. He was confident enough in his analysis that he believed he would eventually be proven correct, and he'd bought himself enough wiggle room (more than enough, in fact) to wait for the market to reward him. However, had he bought with no margin of safety, overpaying for his shares of the Post, he'd be much less certain that any eventual return he might earn on the shares would be thanks to anything more than blind luck—or other suckers willing to pay more than he did. And that would make waiting *much* more nerve-racking.

Calculating a company's intrinsic value, which you need to do before you can start thinking about whether there's an acceptable margin of safety, is a complex task, and one that we won't tackle here. However, there are ample resources available on www.fool.com should you want to investigate further and learn how to put this into action. The main point for now is to understand what it represents and how Buffett employs the concept of margin of safety to limit his risk. Advanced investors and value hounds do the same. Perhaps you're now intrigued enough to join them.

Another way that Buffett shuns risk is found in his attitude toward debt. Given his cautious nature, it's not surprising that he's not a big proponent of debt, whether we're talking about personal debt or debt that Berkshire or other companies have on their books, because of the risk too much debt can bring. The problem with debt is that its overuse can be disastrous when times get rocky. Buying stocks on margin (that is, using borrowed money from your broker), for example, can create trouble when stocks plummet, because your nervous broker is going to want its money back.

Think about credit card debt—the principle's the same. When times are flush, you can use your credit card sensibly, you have no trouble keeping up with your payments, and you can use the credit as it was intended—as a tool but not a crutch. However, one lost job or big uncovered medical bill later, and it's easy to get behind if you've overrelied on credit and run up an unwieldy amount buying faux-mink neck warmers, gold coffee tables, and a fleet of hot-air balloons. It can turn a bad situation into a much worse one (but at least you have your neck warmers to, you know, keep you warm).

The same goes for businesses that borrow money, whether to finance new ventures, build or improve buildings or plants, or pay temporary operating costs. A little debt, managed well, normally won't create havoc. But beware piling it on. Dark times can mean missed payments, which for a company needing loans in the future can mean doubts about its cred-itworthiness. And those doubts register with investors, too, who may flee debt-laden companies for other more cash-rich outfits.

Buffett likes to keep Berkshire as cash rich as possible. In his 2008 letter to shareholders, he wrote, repeating thoughts he'd shared before, "However, I have pledged—to you, the rating agencies and myself—to always run Berkshire with more than ample cash. We never want to count on the kind-ness of strangers in order to meet tomorrow's obligations. When forced to choose, I will not trade even a night's sleep for the chance of extra profits."[4]

It's telling that a master investor such as Buffett refuses to allow Berkshire to take on significant amounts of debt. If he doesn't trust it—and we are talking about the greatest investor of all time here, a mathematical mastermind like no other—then how should the rest of us be approaching the question of debt? It, without a doubt, raises your risk. The safest thing to do, when practicable, is to avoid it like Buffett does.

Buffett also limits his risk exposure by staying within his so-called "sphere of understanding," as we discussed in an ear-lier chapter. By sticking to what he knows, Buffett lowers his risk of a poor decision based on faulty knowledge and assump-tions. That's not to say the man never makes mistakes (we'll get to some of his most notable ones later on), but he does what he can to make as few as possible.

Buffett further manages his risk by investing mostly in companies based in America versus buying foreign stocks. Berkshire's owned shares of various international companies over the years, including the Irish beer business Guinness, the Chinese oil company PetroChina, and a couple of Irish banks.

Berkshire also owns the Israeli automated toolmaker Iscar outright, and has recently owned shares of BYD, a Chinese company that makes batteries, electric cars, and mobile phones. But for the most part, Buffett has stuck close to home.

There are great advantages to investing overseas—you can own shares of newer, faster-growing companies in new markets, for one thing. But there are risks, too. Knowing the geopolitical climate behind every market, as well as differing accounting rules, adds a layer of complexity to investment decisions. For Buffett, for the most part, that's a risk he's chosen to pass on.

All investing involves risk. The quicker you get used to and comfortable with this fact, the better. However, there's no need to take on more risk than is necessary. Follow Buffett's lead here:

- Insist on an appropriate margin of safety.
- Avoid debt as much as possible.
- Stay within your circle of competence.
- Do your homework before investing overseas.

7

Focus on the Positives of Pessimism

Buffett's notoriously optimistic about America, our ability to overcome hardships, and our future. When the markets were roiling in the fall of 2008, and fear and panic were at their height, Buffett became something of a national cheerleader. He wrote an op-ed for the *New York Times* called "Buy American. I Am," in October 2008. In the article, he wrote that amid the chaos, good American companies were selling for such inexpensive prices that he would be buying them for his own personal portfolio—not Berkshire's portfolio, mind you, which already held many great American companies, but his own account, where before this he'd owned only government bonds.[1]

Why would Buffett so boldly declare this "Buy American" sentiment at such a perilous time? Because he believed, in his words, that "fears regarding the long-term prosperity of the nation's many sound companies make no sense."[2] Buffett was decidedly *not* making a "market call," nor predicting that the stock market was going to turn around anytime soon. He very clearly indicated that he had no idea when the market would turn around, only that, eventually, it would. And when it did you wanted to be among the brave investors who bought when times looked bleakest.

Buffett is without a doubt an optimist at heart, but he's smartly recognized and exploited the fact that pessimistic times can create scenarios that lead to great wealth for investors in the long term. That will likely turn out to be the case for investors who listened to Buffett's advice and bought stocks when it seemed the whole world was falling apart around them in the fall of 2008 (and I certainly hope to be in that number). As he said in his *New York Times* piece, echoing thoughts he's shared before, "bad news is an investor's best friend. It lets you buy a slice of America's future at a marked-down price."[3] He's also said, "When investing, pessimism is your friend, euphoria the enemy."[4]

In his 2009 letter to shareholders, Buffett hammered this point again, writing, "A climate of fear is their [investors'] best friend. Those who invest only when commentators are upbeat end up paying a heavy price for meaningless reassurance. In the end, what counts in investing is what you pay for a business—through the purchase of a small piece of it in the stock market—and what that business earns in the succeeding decade or two."[5]

Buffett's careful not to let his inherent optimism cloud his judgment. He remains even-tempered about his investments, and about the market's ups and downs. His mentor Ben Graham talked and wrote about a fictional character named "Mr. Market," who was available to do business with you each day, offering to buy your shares from you or sell you new ones, at varying prices.[6] If you said no to him one day, it was no problem—he'd just return tomorrow with yet another offer. Buffett likes this analogy and has shared it over the years, reminding investors that they remain in charge of Mr. Market—not the other way around. You can't get too worked up about his wishy-washy movements one way or the other.

This attitude is also what lets Buffett avoid periods of hype and hysteria, like the 1990s technology boom. The unlimited optimism that investors saw in technology at that time escaped Buffett. As he wrote in a 1979 article in *Forbes*, "The future is never clear. You pay a very high price in the stock market for a cheery consensus. Uncertainty actually is the friend of the buyer of long-term values."[7]

THE POWER OF PESSIMISM

During an interview conducted in September 2010, Bill Mann of the Motley Fool Independence Fund and the Motley Fool Great America Fund touched on the issue of optimism and pessimism as it applies to value investors:

"When you looked at a company [to value it], you said, 'Well, it earned a dollar this year and I am going to muddle it out at 10 percent growth going on for X period of time.' Whenever I was doing something, there was something in the back of my mind that always said, but what if it doesn't? I think that that is one of the core attributes of value investors.

"If you think about the stock market, the stock market is an exercise in optimism. It is almost an irrational optimism because you are saying whenever you buy something, that you are smarter than the rest of the market. You know more. You have better insight than 100 million people who are willing to buy or sell stocks. I think that is a pretty bold statement for a lot of people. It is a bold statement for everybody.

"So to come into what is an optimistic pursuit and be pessimistic about whatever you are looking at, I think it is a pretty interesting mindset, but I don't know that I have seen too many people in the stock market get in trouble by being too pessimistic. Generally speaking, you see the other side of the coin. People say, 'Well, this company is growing at 40 percent, it is going to keep growing at 40 percent, or if I want to be conservative about it, it is going to just grow at 36 percent.' Well you know, what if it doesn't? What happens then? What is your protection?

"I think that that is really the essence of a value investor—someone who enters into situations where he sees, even if he happens to be wrong because it's not like value investors have some greater insight on the future, but they see some sort of defensive stance, be it just in the utterly low level of the stock price, or there is something about the company that they think people are missing. But you still go through the process of being a pessimistic optimist, I guess would be the least awful way to put it."[8]

Graham's investing philosophy was actually built on pessimism, something that Buffett moved slowly away from over the years. Dubbed "cigar butt" investing, the idea was to find the cheapest stock possible (say, a company selling for below what all of its assets would fetch in the open market), and buy shares in it, hoping to snag a few final puffs from it as you might a discarded cigar you came across on the street. (Yes, yuck.) This school of thought didn't take into account the quality of management, or the company's future prospects, or the strength of its brand or competitive advantage. It was strictly about "margin of safety," as we talked about in the previous chapter.

Graham's style was pessimistic in the sense that you weren't looking for businesses to invest in for the rest of their lives, and your life, benefiting from their moats and appreciating their ability to flourish. No, instead you were merely walking around with your head down, looking for one puff here and one puff there, with no eye to the future, no hope for the business tomorrow and the following day.

Thanks in part to the influence of his business partner, Charlie Munger (we'll delve into this more in a later chapter), Buffett began looking past this pessimism, and looking for businesses that were strong enterprises with bright futures. Nonetheless, he did not allow himself to become blinded by optimism. He remains steadfastly realistic when analyzing companies, hoping for neither pies in the sky, nor cigar butts in the gutter with one remaining puff in them.

To make sure you don't get caught up in unwarranted optimism, remember:

- Be levelheaded about your investments and the market at large. Learn not to be excited by market swings to the upside or devastated by market drops.
- You're in charge of Mr. Market. Don't let him boss you around.
- Quoting Buffett, "When investing, pessimism is your friend, euphoria the enemy."

8

Research Extensively

The "cocktail party" stock tip is something we've all heard about, and maybe even experienced ourselves, delicious pig-in-blanket in hand. Or perhaps your Great-Uncle Irv is always whispering in your ear about that "sure thing" he heard about from his broker while fitting in eighteen holes at the club. And there's certainly never a shortage of expertly coiffed, smartly dressed, and sometimes smart-sounding guys and gals on television telling you what *they* think you should be investing in. While it may be tempting to listen to any or all of them and jump into a stock you know little to nothing about (when has Uncle Irv ever steered you wrong?), resist!

Buffett believes, and you should, too, that you need to put in ample research time before buying shares of a company. It's not enough just to know a ticker symbol; you need to understand what the company does, how it makes its money, and just who is running the show. This level of reconnaissance is a productive means for figuring out if you're looking at an enterprise with a durable competitive advantage and strong moat, or just another here-today-gone-tomorrow pretender. You can't know all that without doing the work, folks. (As a side note, it's amusing to think about how much research someone will do before buying a new computer or car or refrigerator, but when it comes to investing their hard-earned money in public companies—in buying a part of a business, remember—many people are content to listen to others and do as little as possible themselves.)

Luckily, we've got things a whole lot easier than Buffett did back when he first started reading about and researching companies. Thanks to the Internet, the quick, largely free access we have today to financial information is seemingly limitless. Buffett had to go in person to the Securities and Exchange Commission to see company filings. "That was the only way to get them," he's said.[1] It was a similar story for some Moody's and Standard & Poor's reports. He'd have to show up and request the documents he wanted on specific companies from their library, and then sit, going through them bit by bit, taking notes for himself. He didn't even have the benefit of a copy machine![2]

When he wasn't hanging out at Moody's, Standard & Poor's, or the Securities and Exchange Commission in person, Buffett was hauling around those giant Moody's and Standard & Poor's manuals. He started this habit when he was in business school at Columbia, learning from his mentor Ben Graham to dig for potential investments.

These aren't 100-page paperbacks we're talking about, either. Think 10,000 pages for the hardcover *Moody's Manuals*, covering just about every public company under the sun and moon. Buffett has said he went through all the *Moody's Manuals* twice—all 10,000 pages—when he was working as a stockbroker at his father's Omaha firm, looking at each and every business.[3]

Buffett also wasn't above visiting companies in person to learn more about them and talk to management face-to-face. He first did this with GEICO (now owned in full by Berkshire Hathaway) when he was a graduate student. Having heard that Graham's investment firm liked the company, Buffett decided to investigate further. He showed up at GEICO's corporate offices on a Saturday and before long, found himself quizzing a vice president about the company's financials and prospects. Shortly thereafter, Buffett invested a substantial chunk of his money in GEICO's stock.

Buffett's insatiable desire to learn everything and read everything he can get his hands on is legendary. He's an absolute sponge, soaking up far more information than seems humanly possible. He devours annual reports, business magazines, and books aplenty. He reportedly reads at least five newspapers a day, and has been reading the *Wall Street Journal* daily since he was in college.[4] In fact, once he was living and working back in Omaha he arranged to have the *Journal* delivered early to his office each morning, so he'd have a jump on everyone else when it came to the latest financial news.[5]

Buffett's days in his modest Omaha office are usually spent reading, from the time he gets in until the time he heads home. He reads about seven hundred annual reports a year, taking forty-five minutes to read each one cover to cover. Talk about using your time wisely! He has optimized this time-consuming process perfectly. Given that he's mostly just sitting around reading all day, he's talked before about how boring his time at the office would look to an outsider. (Although I have to say, as someone who absolutely loves to read, this sounds pretty heavenly to me.)

His nights typically aren't that different. His three adult

children have talked about their father's reading habits when they were growing up; he'd go up to his study upstairs after supper and read until he went to sleep—they knew not to disturb him unless absolutely necessary.[6] Buffett is simply driven to absorb as much knowledge and information as he can.

One benefit from this is that he can often make complex financial decisions faster than most of us—math whizzes or no—would feel comfortable doing. Because he's spent so much time learning in detail about the financials of nearly every company he might feasibly be interested in owning, he can quickly assess potential deals. About his ongoing prep work, Buffett has reportedly said, "Noah did not start building the Ark when it was raining."[7] Buffett reads to stay ready for new business propositions in addition to keeping up with the financials of Berkshire's current holdings.

Buffett's mind is razor sharp and his power to recall information is astonishing. Andrew Kilpatrick, author of *Of Permanent Value: The Story of Warren Buffett,* says that "he is in fact a genius and the rest of us mortals can't relate to that. If you tell people he can read and absorb a book in one sitting, people don't believe it because they can't do it."[8]

But while it certainly helps, you don't have to possess his remarkable intellect and near-perfect memory to succeed as an investor. (Thank goodness! Most of us would be sadly out of luck were these traits nonnegotiable requirements. And remember, too, what Buffett himself said about temperament trumping IQ in investing.)

You *do* need to crave knowledge as he does, though. It's not necessary to request early delivery of the *Wall Street Journal,* or read five newspapers a day, or spend your evenings at home holed up with a stack of annual reports. You've likely got other things to attend to, right? But to become a better investor, you've got to become a lover of businesses and a better scholar.

You've got to learn the basics of accounting, so you'll know your way around a balance sheet, for instance, and won't be flummoxed when someone's talking about accounts receivable or goodwill. You've got to read about different business models, to understand how they make money.

How is discount giant Wal-Mart's approach different from jewelry store Tiffany's, for example? They're both retailers, but they practice very different approaches to business. The answer? Wal-Mart sells a whole lot of things with very little markup, a high volume/low margin strategy, while Tiffany chooses to sell fewer, higher-quality items but makes more money off each one. (Oh, and naturally, there's the fact that Wal-Mart doesn't use those cute little robin's egg blue boxes and doesn't have a legendary movie with its name in the title starring the one and only Audrey Hepburn. But I digress.)

You've got to become comfortable with the peculiar language of business, and to get there, you've got to embrace reading about it. Having a healthy curiosity about the world around you helps. Buffett's eternally curious, and this is a huge asset for him. You can never be sure where your next great investment idea or possibility is going to come from. Being open to learning about anything and everything provides you with the mental makeup to embrace new ideas.

THE BENEFITS OF BEING CURIOUS AND WELL-READ

Lisa Rapuano, founder of Lane Five Capital Management, has as one of her firm's core values, "Learn and read widely." In a September 2010 interview, she elaborated on why this is so important:

"It matters because the world is complex and the world is adaptive. I don't know why this is, I don't have a theological or epistemological foundation for this, but it has come to my attention time and time again that there are patterns in the world that repeat across seemingly unrelated systems. So there are things about the markets that appear to me to be very similar to the way that biological systems work. Or there are analogies, there are recurring patterns that are similar, and we sure know a lot more about biological systems than we do about the markets, and so if I can study biological systems and they can give me any little insight into how this works, that's helpful. And it's really indirect, so I don't want to make it sound like, 'Well I study nerve systems and I figure out that this works that way.' It's really very indirect and very amorphous.

"There's also the element of historical patterns, not just systems, but events, such as the way that wars happen, the way that cultures evolve, the way that demographics have affected countries, the way that natural events have affected countries—again, amorphous, indirect, but they provide greater connections in your brain, your brain becomes more robust, and the pattern recognition machine becomes better. You make connections that other people might not make. That's at a very broad level.

"At a more practical level, a curious person is more likely to uncover the piece of information that will be the evidence you need to have higher confidence than the next guy that is not curious enough to be resourceful. You know, someone who's basically like, 'I get this. I understand how this works. I don't need to think about it all that much.' Whereas someone like me, or the people who work for me, are always asking, 'How else can I think of that? What am I missing? What else is happening? What else could I do? How else could I turn this on its head? What else could I research to figure out if this is right or not?'

"Now, you have to be careful with that, because you could work on one thing twelve hours a day for the rest of your life and still not have 100 percent information. But it's the drive to be curious, and the person who naturally wants to learn and read widely is more likely to be a better analyst. Then, secondly, the act of reading widely and broadly provides you with a more robust set of patterns and connections and networks that, at the margin, I think help you understand how the world works."[9]

Now, this isn't to say that Buffett's going to spend a lot of time—nor should you—reading about and following in detail the companies that lie outside his circle of competence. As we talked about earlier, he very clearly defines which industries and types of companies fall into his circle and then he sticks to it. Thanks to his curiosity, it's not a stretch to imagine him keeping up with some companies that fall outside his circle in a peripheral kind of way, but not with the same depth and intensity he devotes to the companies he fully understands.

As we found earlier, because of the fast-moving and ever-changing nature of technology, for example, Buffett doesn't feel comfortable trying to predict their future cash flows. It's unlikely, then, that he's spending a significant amount of time reading about tech companies, outside of some of the biggies that we know fascinate him like Microsoft and Google. His research time and brainpower are better focused elsewhere. This is a lesson for us, as well. Unless you are certain that diving deep into new areas is going to bring them within your circle of competence, you are probably better served by continuing to learn as much as you can and deepening your knowledge about the industries and companies you are already comfortable with.

Another key asset for Buffett is his ability to avoid what's known as "confirmation bias," the very human tendency to seek out only information that confirms a conclusion we've arrived at, versus challenging it.[10] We're biased toward news that pleases us; question us, and not so much. It's the grown-up equivalent of sticking your fingers in your ears and yelling nonsense when you don't want to hear what someone's telling you.

However, avoiding negative information can be deadly for investors. Letting confirmation bias rule your investment decisions can compound mistakes, because it can make you unwilling to admit you made one in the first place. As we'll see later in our chapter on mistakes, Buffett is uncannily good at admitting he's made them. It may hurt his ego, it may upset him, but when new information presents itself that disproves something he believed, he analyzes it and accepts it. Writing about a purchase he made of oil company ConocoPhillips when oil prices were sky-high and then subsequently plummeted, he says, "so far I have been dead wrong. Even if prices should rise, moreover, the terrible timing of my purchase has cost Berkshire several billion dollars."[11]

When you don't take the time to question your thinking, to consider what could go wrong, to noodle on what you could be missing in your analysis, you automatically increase your risk. And we know that Buffett believes you should do everything you possibly can to *reduce* your risk. Making sure you've considered alternate points of view helps you do this. You won't be perfect at it; no one is. But trying to think about all points of view—not just the ones that indicate you're right—is tremendously helpful.

Writing in his 2008 letter to Berkshire Hathaway shareholders about the human inclination to want approval for one's investment ideas, Buffett said, "Approval, though, is not the goal of investing. In fact, approval is often counter-productive because it sedates the brain and makes it less receptive to new facts or a re-examination of conclusions formed earlier. Beware the investment activity that produces applause; the great moves are usually greeted by yawns."[12]

So, in order to get the most out of the time you spend researching (a real necessity to becoming a great investor):

- Read, read, read. (You can check the appendix in the back for a list of books, if you want a place to start.)
- Don't forget about your circle of competence.
- Avoid confirmation bias—actively seek out information that contradicts your conclusions, not only information that reinforces them.

9

Ignore Peer Pressure

Buffett's primary investment principles were solidified early in life, thanks to his mentor Ben Graham. Though Buffett evolved his thinking somewhat over the years, incorporating ideas about more qualitative investing from business partner Charlie Munger and growth investing pioneer Philip Fisher (we'll get into this further later on), once he'd formed his philosophical foundation, he never wavered from it.

Buffett would encounter trying periods for his intellectual strength and psychological fortitude in just about every decade he's been investing in. He's been seen as "out of step" (his own words in a 1967 letter to his partners) or past his prime, time and time again.[1] Pundits have derided his opposition to technology investments, declaring him washed up, his style of investing no longer successful.

Before he was the well-known Buffett of magazine covers and book titles (ahem), he faced pricey, irrational markets that left him little choice but to wait with cash burning a hole in his proverbial pocket. Through it all, through the criticism, through the frustration of seeing good companies simply selling for too high a price, Buffett stayed true to himself, certain in his beliefs. He did not abandon his Graham-based ideology, and he did not doubt that the way he was investing was the best and most sensible way to go about things.

In a televised November 2009 CNBC interview Buffett participated in (along with Bill Gates) at Columbia University, he said, "Having sound principles takes you through everything. And the bedrock principles that really I learned from Graham and Dodd, I haven't had to do anything with them. They take me through good periods, they take me through bad periods. In the end, I don't worry about them because I know they work."[2]

The Buffett partnership began in 1956, and he quickly and easily found undervalued places to invest his partners' money. However, as the 1960s progressed, dubbed the "Go-Go" years by market hotshots making fast, easy money, Buffett found himself frustrated, with too much money to invest and too few opportunities to do so. Indeed, in 1966 he closed his partnership to new investors.

At the time, predating another tech bubble that would see Buffett's logic questioned, investors were snapping up technology and electronics companies without pausing to ask exactly what these companies did or how they made money.

Buffett refused to participate in the madness, telling his partners in the aforementioned 1967 letter to them, "When the game is no longer being played your way, it is only human to say the new approach is all wrong, bound to lead to trouble, etc. I have been scornful of such behavior by others in the past. I have also seen the penalties incurred by those who evaluate conditions as they were—not as they are. Essentially, I am out of step with present conditions. On one point, however, I am clear. I will not abandon a previous approach whose logic I understand even though it may mean forgoing large, and apparently easy, profits to embrace an approach which I don't fully understand, have not practiced successfully and which, possibly, could lead to substantial permanent loss of capital."[3] (It should be pointed out, however, that thanks to his earlier purchases, the partnership performed very well in the 1960s. He closed the partnership in 1969, having given his lucky partners a 32 percent average annual return before fees.)

From this point early in his career, Buffett had to be strong and not bend to mob rule. Sure, he could have followed all the other "investors" (Buffett likely wouldn't agree with that characterization of them) into the market, hopping into stocks that he didn't understand but were nevertheless going up because everyone else was in a frenzy, but that is not who he is or how he operates. He believes in being systematic and having a set approach, a framework, and once you know who you are as an investor and what you're looking for, you stick to it. Changing with every market whim and speculative wind that blows through Wall Street is not the way to build wealth over the long term.

Buffett would be tested again in the early 1970s, as mutual fund managers poured money into a group of big companies known as the "Nifty Fifty." The fact that everyone was doing it was not enough reason for Buffett to join them, and he set out on his own, snapping up cheap shares of companies other investors were ignoring. The stock market swooned in 1973–74, and despite his current investments losing value, Buffett was excited about the chance to pick up companies he believed in for ever-lower prices. The more dismal the stock market became, the happier it made Buffett.

The 1960s and the 1970s were, together, periods that

exemplified one of Buffett's most famous sayings: "Be fearful when others are greedy, and greedy when others are fearful." In the 1960s, there had been euphoria and greed galore, and Buffett patiently waited on the sidelines, hesitant to join the sure-to-end party. Then, as the market collapsed in the mid-1970s, and most investors were all filled up with fear, Buffett was greedily adding to his favorite positions and initiating new ones.

When interviewed by *Forbes* magazine in 1974, and asked how he felt about the stock market at that particular time, Buffett said, "Like an oversexed guy in a harem. This is the time to start investing." (OK, so clearly Buffett does have *some* traces of testosterone.) He added, "Now is the time to invest and get rich."[4] This attitude and ability to remain cool in the face of panic and market declines is a trait that separates Buffett; it's also something you've got to learn to develop in order to be a better investor.

Speaking of Buffett and his remarkable temperament, Roger Lowenstein, author of *Buffett: The Making of an American Capitalist*, and more recently, *The End of Wall Street*, said in an interview published on Fool.com, "How many times have we heard he's through? We heard that in the dot.com era and we heard it in the mortgage era again. Just bubble after bubble, he stands on the sidelines and lets other people take what seem to be easy gains until they come crashing down. It sounds easy in retrospect, but it just takes an awful lot of self-confidence."[5]

Lowenstein also said, "The key to his temperament is that he is comfortable following his own instincts and judgment and ignoring (when he disagrees with it) that of the consensus. This has enabled him to avoid many, many investment fads and perils over the course of his career, from the Go-Go stocks of the '60s to the Nifty Fifty of the early '70s, to the dot.coms of the late '90s and the mortgage bubble of recent years."[6]

It can be incredibly scary to go against what other investors are doing. To be contrarian is so difficult. The conviction in your own analysis and beliefs is paramount. Otherwise, you might as well give in, give up, and resign yourself to a future following the so-called herd, investing in what everyone else is, destined to do only as well as they do.

DON'T WAVER FROM YOUR CONVICTIONS

In an interview, value investor and founder of Paradigm Capital Management Candace King Weir said of the challenge of staying true to yourself, "you have to have a certain set courage of your own convictions, because often you can be wrong for weeks or months. It's not that you really were wrong, but you appear to be wrong. . . . So you do have to have the courage of your convictions, I think to be good. You really have to be grounded.

"I think we had a pretty fabulous year in '09, just because we stuck to our knitting when other people were just frozen in the ground. We'd just come in and we'd talk to our companies and if we thought that things were really outrageously out of whack, then we would buy a little more, but fundamentally we are very disciplined. I think discipline is really critical, too. You do have to show up every day, no matter the days you hate it. You say, 'I can't bear it.' You can't bear to lose any more money. I take it very personally always, but if you don't show up, you don't get to play the game and eventually you are just out of the game."[7]

Let's not fool ourselves. Overcoming this tendency is ridiculously hard. Recent research even shows that when we conform, the areas of our brain that are activated are the same ones associated with pleasure.[8] So, truly, piling in behind other investors, and having them pile in behind us, actually, literally feels really good. But remember, as Buffett has said, "Approval . . . is not the goal of investing."[9]

Instead, a carefully calculated weighing of the facts, and of your analysis of the company's future prospects, is called for. When everyone in the market believes something's true, ask yourself what they're missing. Question the conclusions of pundits. Don't assume that they know more than you do, or know something you don't. The best place to look for promising investments is often the very place most investors have turned their backs on. Look where others aren't looking.

When Buffett was just a young graduate student and visited the Washington, D.C., headquarters of GEICO in person and ended up investing three-quarters of his portfolio in the company, he did so based on his own analysis of the company. He didn't listen to anyone else. Even his mentor Ben Graham would have believed he was overpaying, and yet Buffett so trusted himself that he forged ahead.[10] He didn't let self-doubt take over.

Developing this ability to control your emotions takes time and work. For Buffett, it seems to be innate, though he's had to endure ridicule time and again for missing out on big market movements. The dramatic late 1990s–early 2000 rise in the market at large, and in technology and Internet companies in particular, was one such time.

In 1999 alone, the Dow Jones Industrial Average rose 25 percent, while the tech-heavy Nasdaq rocketed ahead a remarkable 86 percent. Meanwhile, Buffett sat on the sidelines, certain that the market's rise was founded on nothing more than unicorns, rainbows, and that little puppy dog sock puppet from Pets.com. He most certainly did not purchase shares of Internet companies for Berkshire, leaving the easy money to everyone else, and he was questioned for it. Buffett endured doubts about his investing abilities and method for several years during this period. Berkshire's stock price suffered, too, giving even more ammunition to the media proclaiming Buffett's best days behind him. The criticism was loud and unrelenting.

It's not easy being misunderstood, or worse, mocked, but the Oracle stood strong. Talking in an interview about that time, Buffett said, "You can't do well in investing unless you think independently. And the truth is, you are neither right nor wrong because people agree with you. You're right because your facts and reasoning are right. In the end, that's what counts."[11]

And, of course, in the end Buffett *was* right. Investing hadn't changed overnight. Value still mattered. The way to build wealth over the long term wasn't, in fact, found by throwing money at anything and everything ending in a ".com." But it was most likely trying for Buffett to hear and absorb the blows. It will be trying for you, too, at times, but if you've developed your investing philosophy appropriately, you've got to also develop the self-confidence—and thick skin—to stick with it.

STAY TRUE TO YOURSELF

Lisa Rapuano, founder of Lane Five Capital Management, understands how difficult it can be for investors to shut out criticism. In a September 2010 interview, she said, "When you're not doing well,

in the shorter term, which can happen to anyone, sometimes it's because you're making mistakes, sometimes it's because you're not applying your process correctly, but sometimes you are and you still
aren't doing well. You have to combine these two things of being
adaptive, open-minded, and being a learning machine with also not
changing your stripes or chasing the latest trend. It's a really fine line,
a really difficult line to walk."[12]

Buffett has demonstrated his ability to withstand peer
pressure at other times, too. During the market's 22.6 percent
one-day crash in October 1987, Buffett didn't bow to fear and
run away from stocks. The same goes for the period in late
2001 and early 2002 when news of the massive accounting
fraud at Enron and other companies broke, creating investors'
distrust in management and reported financial results. Suddenly every public company and executive was suspect. Buffett looked at the conditions created by all that nervousness
and took advantage of it. He's said, "Cash combined with courage in a crisis is priceless."[13]

More recently, and as we talked about earlier, Buffett
again showed his courage in the panic-ridden fall of 2008 as
the market, and seemingly the world, tumbled around him.
He became the reassuring voice in the dark night that investors needed, publishing his *New York Times* editorial to encourage others to be brave and take a stand as he was.[14] Buffett
would follow through on his words, too, investing in Goldman
Sachs and General Electric at this time, although it must be
said that he did negotiate very favorable deals when he made
these two investments, setting them up as preferred stock
deals that ensured Berkshire a certain return. Most investors

couldn't have gotten the deals on these companies that Buffett did (indeed it's hard to imagine anyone *but* Buffett exacting the terms he did), but that doesn't diminish the fact that he was acting as a model of investment temperament at the time.

It's possible to practice being "greedy when others are fearful and fearful when others are greedy" both when the market as a whole is in decline, and at the individual company level. Buffett has done it both ways, targeting companies that are temporarily down because investors misunderstand or doubt their future earning potential (as he did when he picked up shares of the Washington Post in the 1970s with a generous margin of safety) or jumping into the market and snapping up shares of many desirable businesses when everyone else seems to have run off, leaving cheap stocks scattered about like abandoned toys.

Another way that Buffett asserts his independence and won't bow to peer pressure is his stance on dividends and stock splits. Aside from one $0.10 per share dividend paid by Berkshire way back in 1967 (Buffett joked "I must have been in the bathroom" when the decision was made to pay a dividend),[15] Buffett has denied paying anything out to Berkshire stockholders. The reason's simple: He believes that Berkshire shareholders are better served by him hanging on to the money and investing it back into Berkshire's stable of wholly owned and partially owned companies versus paying them out a dividend. There are also tax implications with paying dividends, both at the company level and at the individual shareholder level, but that's not Buffett's primary concern.

To Buffett, the way a business chooses to allocate its capital is the most important thing. If you can efficiently and effectively allocate your capital into profitable new lines of business or in improving existing business lines, then you shouldn't be paying a dividend. But that's a big *if*. If a business is mature and not growing rapidly, and management's ability to allocate capital is constrained, shareholders deserve to have that money paid out to them to compensate for the likely lack of growth in the stock price.

In Berkshire's case, though, we can agree that Buffett is a master capital allocator, and it's a pretty safe bet that he can do more with the excess money generated by the company's insurance operations than his shareholders could. He is, after all, Warren Buffett. Nevertheless, certain investors and segments of the market crave dividends for income and have been disappointed with Buffett's stance. It's logical, though, and is fully consistent with his beliefs.

Of course, there is always the possibility that Berkshire's immense size will truly catch up with it and create a situation where paying out a dividend actually does make more sense than retaining all the earnings, but so far, that hasn't happened. Buffett's been warning about the drag Berkshire's size has on its results for years, and at some point that could make his current stand on dividends more difficult to rationally defend. We'll see.

Buffett has also long held the belief that stock splits are pointless and a waste of time, money, and energy. In a stock split, the overall amount your shares are worth doesn't change, but the number of shares you own does. So, for instance, if you owned 5 shares at $4 each of Big Al's Corndog Emporium and the company splits its stock 2-for-1, you'd then own 10 shares at $2 per share. Either way, your investment is worth $20 (and those darn dogs are so delicious it's likely to keep going up).

Companies split their stock for all sorts of reasons, none of which are particularly compelling to Buffett. Some say it's to help create more "liquidity" and make it easier for more investors to purchase the company's shares. This has certainly been an argument presented as a reason Buffett should split the "A" shares of Berkshire Hathaway. Trading at a price of around or above $100,000 for one share (!) of stock, Berkshire is out of the reasonable price range for many investors.

Buffett, though, doesn't believe splitting Berkshire's stock would have any positive effect on the company or its owners and indeed, could even create a group of shareholders that he deems undesirable. Buffett wants Berkshire to have long-term-focused shareholders (he refers to them as "partners"), and he wants Berkshire's price to reflect the company's intrinsic value as closely as possible. Splitting the stock would create the potential for irrational stock movements caused by new speculative shareholders focused on the short term.

However, Buffett's hand was forced on the stock split issue in the mid-1990s. Investment houses, wise to the fact that more people wanted to own a piece of Berkshire Hathaway than could afford one, planned to buy shares of Berkshire and divvy them up, selling them as smaller units to the public, and charging fat fees for the privilege. To avoid what he saw as an expensive and unfair way to profit from Berkshire's success at the expense of small investors, Buffett created a second class of Berkshire shares in 1996, the "B" shares, which were valued at 1/30 of an "A" share and had voting rights of 1/200 of an "A" share.

The Berkshire "B" shares, however, *were* actually split 50-to-1 in early 2010, to help shareholders of Burlington Northern, which Berkshire announced it intended to purchase in full at the end of 2009. Burlington shareholders could choose either cash or Berkshire stock, so by making the share price lower for them, Buffett made it easier for them to choose the stock versus the cash (and avoid any nasty tax implications). This move also opened the door for Berkshire to replace Burlington Northern in the S&P 500 (can you believe it wasn't already in there?).

You have to believe, though, that Buffett's thinking on the silliness of stock splits hasn't changed. Unusual circumstances forced him to both create the B shares back in the 1990s and then split them more recently. His desire to have long-term shareholders/partners remains as real today as ever. He did what he did with the B shares because he was looking out for the best interests of small, individual investors, not because he suddenly decided everyone was right about stock splits.

Reputation is a significant matter for Buffett, which is another reason he is unlikely to bend to peer pressure. If there's a risk it could sully his reputation, Buffett won't have any part of it. He once famously told his oldest son, "It takes twenty years to build a reputation and five minutes to ruin it. If you think about that you'll do things differently." [16]

Buffett believes in something he's dubbed the "Inner Scorecard." [17] Essentially, it's a framework for living your life according to your own rules and your own beliefs, and not acting according to whether or not other people will approve of you. For Buffett, naturally, this encompasses financial decision making. You have to be able to tune out the world and live by your Inner Scorecard.

To be a great investor, you've got to go it alone, at least to a certain extent. You can learn from the masters, as Buffett did (and, well, as you are now doing reading this very book), but in the end, you've got to develop your own system for investing. And then you've got to stick to it. Don't abandon your beliefs when times get harrowing. Ask the hard questions. Ask the next question. And then act, or don't act, as appropriate.

Buffett's had a long time to perfect this part of his temperament, and it is key to what has made him as successful as he's been. So keep at it, stay strong, and go your own way. Keep the following in mind as you commence your journey:

- Be willing to be contrarian, as uncomfortable as it may be.
- Take Buffett's words to heart: "Be greedy when others are fearful, and fearful when others are greedy."
- Live by your own Inner Scorecard.

10

Learn from Mistakes

Buffett is legendary, without a doubt, but he's also not perfect. He makes mistakes just like the rest of us, and he's remarkably good about admitting them and analyzing them after the fact to see what can be learned (typically in his own very funny and self-effacing way in his annual shareholder letters). He's able to set ego aside for a rational look at what went wrong.

This trait is invaluable for investors; knowing what you did wrong and doing everything you can to avoid repeating it helps preserve precious capital and improve your returns over the long term. There are times where you're going to do your analysis, make your decision, and either something changes that renders your conclusion null, or you will have simply made a mistake somewhere in your thinking. It happens to everyone. Like risk, mistakes are an unavoidable part of investing, so it's best to learn to embrace the lessons that can come from them.

Buffett breaks down his mistakes into mistakes of commission, meaning actions he took that didn't turn out as he'd hoped, and mistakes of omission, or actions that he regretted *not* taking. Buffett has said that he's more bothered by his mistakes of omission than the mistakes he's actually made, however.

One mistake of omission Buffett has copped to involves retail giant Wal-Mart. In the 1990s, because he wanted to buy shares of Wal-Mart at a particular price and didn't want to budge from that, he let a one-eighth-of-a-point uptick in the company's stock price prevent him from purchasing it. Over the long run, he estimates that one mistake cost him $10 billion in potential profits.[1] Ouch. That's quite an expensive omission indeed.

Buffett has said that the first mistake of his investing career was the actual purchase of Berkshire Hathaway itself. When he first started buying shares of the company way back in 1962, it was a textile mill, hanging on to its last gasps as a functioning enterprise. Affected as many manufacturers were by cheap overseas competition, Buffett would try unsuccessfully to turn the business around, until he finally closed its textile operations altogether in 1985. By that point, he'd already begun his strategy of buying insurance companies and using the associated float to invest, under the umbrella of Berkshire, so the transformation of the company was well on its way, despite the floundering manufacturing business.

The frustration Buffett may have felt about Berkshire, and the opportunity cost of having his money tied up in trying to save a losing enterprise, are unfortunate, but this is one mistake that he ended up making right. Berkshire may not have been providing much in the way of suit linings (one of its main offerings) by the time Buffett came along, but it ended up providing him, and his shareholders, an investing vehicle that remains unparalleled. And besides, the names Warren Buffett and Berkshire Hathaway just fit so well together, don't they? Can you imagine it any other way?

Another of Buffett's most famous errors is one that provides him the chance in his shareholder letters and in interviews to flog himself for his "Air-aholism." That mistake is investing in the airline US Airways. Buffett invested in the company in 1989, buying what are known as "convertible preferred shares." Basically, this means that Berkshire was promised a fat dividend, and could convert its preferred shares into common stock if it so chose at a certain price. At the time of the investment, US Airways was threatened by a takeover attempt, so Berkshire stepping in and investing money in the company was seen as a form of protection for it.

However, nearly from the get-go US Airways (which was officially named just "US Air" until 1996) plagued Buffett. He was blunt about his mistake in his letters to shareholders over the years he was invested in it, calling his analysis of it "superficial and wrong"[2] and referring to his decision to invest as an "unforced error."

Buffett has written of the investment, "Before this purchase, I simply failed to focus on the problems that would inevitably beset a carrier whose costs were both high and extremely difficult to lower."[3] And he "overlooked the crucial point: US Air's revenues would increasingly feel the effects of an unregulated, fiercely competitive market where its cost structure was a holdover from the days when regulation protected profits. These costs, if left unchecked, portended disaster, however reassuring the airline's past record might be."[4]

There are several interesting things about Berkshire's, and Buffett's, investment in US Airways. One is that it came about at a time when Buffett was having trouble finding other opportunities, so he made the mistake of essentially lowering his standards to invest in it.[5] One mistake begat another, you could say.

Next, while the investment troubled him and worried him, Berkshire actually ended up making money on the deal, thanks both to the return from the dividends and the fact that shares of US Airways eventually got back to about where he'd invested, so he cashed out. Now, granted, had Buffett chosen to deploy his capital elsewhere, he might well have earned a higher return, but US Airways did not, in the end, turn out to be the supreme disaster it looked like it might be.

An additional and important point for us here is that despite the fact that Buffett ultimately made money on US Airways, he still recognizes it as a mistake. His outcome might not have been bad, but his thinking and his decision-making process were. He is able, then, to separate the "outcome" from the "decision." Many investors struggle with this, believing, for example, that their worst-performing stocks represent their worst decisions, and vice versa. But a bad decision does not always turn into a bad outcome, and sometimes good outcomes are actually born of bad decision making. Buffett never fooled himself into believing that US Airways was anything other than a mistake, good outcome or no.

Finally, while Berkshire Hathaway is no longer invested in US Airways, it still has a piece of the air travel industry with its wholly owned subsidiary NetJets. NetJets allows people to buy a part of a private jet (known as "fractional ownership") so that you get the benefit of having a plane all to yourself without the cost of, well, maintaining a plane all by yourself.

However, NetJets hasn't proven to be a big winner for Buffett, and he's written about it much as he did US Airways, noting that he should have called the "Air-aholics hotline" before investing in it. He's also said, hilariously, that someone would have done capitalists a favor if they'd just shot down the Wright brothers in Kitty Hawk that fateful day (because over its history the airline industry has reported zero profits in the aggregate).[6] In his 2009 shareholder letter, he again revisited the topic, expressing his frustration with NetJets but pointing out that he'd made a management change at the top he was optimistic could correct course for the troubled company and turn around its years of losses.[7]

One lesson here for the rest of us is that even someone as talented as Buffett not only makes mistakes, but sometimes makes them more than once. When it comes to this particular one, Buffett has said, "If only women could be CEOs of companies that flew planes I think it would be a lot better," after he came to the conclusion that testosterone was responsible for "Air-aholism."[8]

In Buffett's early days, he partnered with Charlie Munger to buy a Baltimore department store that had seen better times. The store was called Hochschild-Kohn, and returning it to its former glory was an expensive and likely impossible task. As with US Airways, Buffett invested in this business when he was sitting on cash, impatiently looking for stocks to buy in a market that was running away from him.[9] Pretty quickly, both Buffett and Munger realized that they'd made a mistake and that retail was no easy feat. After three years of giving it a go, they subsequently sold Hochschild-Kohn to another buyer for roughly what they had paid, to relieve themselves of the burden. While Buffett and Munger's first deal together looked like an inauspicious beginning, they've certainly managed to overcome this early stumble with impressive force.

The US Airways mistake and the Hochschild-Kohn one have two things in common. First, as mentioned, Buffett invested in both of these companies during periods where he was having trouble finding good companies selling at reasonable prices that he wanted to buy. Instead of being patient, he let his trigger finger get the best of him, and so he ended up jumping into businesses he otherwise should have avoided. It can be challenging even for him to do the right thing, which is to wait it out.

NOBODY ESCAPES MISTAKES

Yes, even successful value investors like Lisa Rapuano make mistakes. We all do. It's just part and parcel of investing. It's something you've got to learn to deal with in order to be successful.

In a September 2010 interview about the lessons she learned from one 2008 trade gone bad involving an auto company, Rapuano said, "The two things I did in that mistake that absolutely drive me to distraction are No. 1, I normally save myself from massive errors like bankruptcy and things like that by avoiding businesses like car businesses. I will do turnarounds, I will do messy things, but I don't usually do *that*. As I look back on it, I think probably because things that appeared cheap to me at that point were few and far between, at the beginning of '08, I overdid it on this one. I put way too much of my portfolio in it because it was so cheap and it was so easily explainable. So it was putting too much in it, in a business that wasn't a good business, so when you are wrong you don't get saved by the goodness of the business.

"And here's the additional lesson—probably the one that's going to be the easiest never to repeat again—I got so much positive feedback on this one. Everyone said it was brilliant. I presented it at the Value Investing Congress and the whole world was like, 'Oh my God, that's the best idea.' I'd talk about it in client meetings and they'd be like, 'Oh it's so great. It's so wonderful. You're going to make a lot of money on this.' It was too easy by half.

"Letting your confidence be affected by other people's reaction to it should have been a giant red flag because normally when I invest in something, especially at the beginning, not after it starts working, everyone thinks I'm wrong. No one ever tells me how great it is.

"There's a lot of little lessons in there, but the big one I think is that external reinforcement of the idea doesn't make it better. And therefore I probably didn't recognize the imperfections of it. I got overconfident. And we just did terribly. It was awful. Even if it hadn't been going into 2008—so let's take that piece out of it, which is a whole 'nother can of worms—[there was] the overconfidence in a bad business and too large a position. Part of our process is avoiding the things where if you're wrong, the business doesn't help you, and actually hurts you, the nature of the business itself hurts you. It was just stupid."[10]

As Berkshire has grown in size at an astounding rate, Buffett's been faced more and more with this problem—he often has too much cash and too few places to put it. (Oh, we should all be so tortured, eh?) The market's overall behavior actually doesn't even matter that much for Berkshire at this point. Certainly it's better for Buffett if stocks are trading for rational prices, but it's Berkshire's cash coffers that make it difficult for him to invest when and where he wants. Berkshire's just too big for him to buy meaningful amounts of stock in any companies but the very largest ones at this point, because for them to have any effect on overall results, he can't just nibble here and there.

As a side point, this is an enormous advantage that you, as an individual investor without the burden of billions of dollars in your bank account and on your balance sheet, have over Warren Buffett. You can find the small, undiscovered, undercover companies that Buffett wouldn't be able to touch, and you can purchase as many shares of them as you want. You can go places he can't in the market and look at opportunities he only wishes he could own a part of. So, see, being a billionaire and holding a spot on *Forbes*'s richest people in the world list (a top 5 spot, to boot) isn't all that great after all. (Ha.)

But back to Buffett's mistakes. The second thing that US Airways and Hochschild-Kohn have in common is that neither one seems particularly "Buffett-like." Neither one seems to have the traits we associate with Buffett today and have already talked about here. There's no moat to speak of in either the airline business (can you say "the very definition of commodity"?) or the department store business. There are no sustainable competitive advantages with either one. US Airways was also a very capital-intensive business, and while Hochschild-Kohn was less so, when Buffett and Munger invested it still needed lots of improvements to its stores to have any hope of remaining relevant and competitive. Both of the businesses can be described as cash-hungry, not cash-producing. And Buffett is all about the cash-producing companies in the world.

So when he was impatient, and wanting to invest his money somewhere, Buffett both lowered his standards and he chose, in these two cases, companies outside what we think of as ideal Buffett investments. US Airways and Hochschild-Kohn are hardly Coca-Cola or GEICO or See's Candies or American Express. Staying patient and waiting for the famed "fat pitch" is so important. But even Buffett is fallible here. Should you make a similar mistake, don't panic. Remember to recognize that you acted when you shouldn't have and then do your best to stick to a vow not to do it again.

Buffett made two more recent mistakes, both of which could be considered errors in his analysis of the companies and their current and future prospects, and both of which cost Berkshire money. As we mentioned earlier, in 2008 he invested in oil giant ConocoPhillips, thinking that the price of oil would rise. Instead, thanks in part to the financial panic later in that same year, the price of oil dropped, and along with it, ConocoPhillips' stock price, which was down 37 percent at the end of 2008 from where Buffett purchased shares.[11]

Around the same time that Berkshire invested in Conoco-Phillips, it also bought shares of two Irish banks. Buffett never disclosed publicly precisely which ones were purchased, but his thinking back then was likely that Irish banks weren't exposed to as much subprime mortgage risk as U.S. banks were, and so they were safer bets at a time when many American banks were going to pieces. Buffett was wrong, and many Irish banks were absolutely slaughtered in the market, with the Irish government even nationalizing some of them. He fessed up to his shareholders about it, disclosing that Berkshire had to write down the value of those two trades to the tune of an 89 percent loss.[12] (I myself succumbed to the faulty thinking about Irish banks around this same time, and watched as the shares I purchased in one of them—perhaps one of the very ones Buffett bought—plummeted about the same amount Berkshire's did. Blimey!)

Here we have two cases of the macroeconomic picture changing so quickly that Buffett's analysis was turned on its head. Sometimes your thinking, analysis, and objective look at the facts, and your projections for the company's future, can be right, but your investments can still turn out wrong. That's disheartening, yes, but it's also just a reality of investing you need to prepare yourself for. You won't always be perfect, even if your analysis is. You can't know every single thing there is to know about a company, and you can't predict the future with absolute certainty—not even Buffett can. (The world's just a cold, cruel place, isn't it?)

Writing of his learning curve in an annual letter to Berkshire shareholders, Buffett said, "It's far better to buy a wonderful company at a fair price than a fair company at a wonderful price. Charlie [Munger] understood this early; I was a slow learner. But now, when buying companies or common stocks, we look for first-class businesses accompanied by first-class managements. That leads right to a related lesson: Good jockeys will do well on good horses but not on broken-down nags."[13]

Even Buffett had to learn from his mistakes over the years, and he's still learning today. The learning never stops, of course. To get the most out of your mistakes, and do your best to ensure they won't happen again, remember:

- You're going to make mistakes. We all do. So don't beat yourself up when you slip up.
- Assess what happened. Did you miss something? Or did market conditions change?
- Think about what you can reasonably do differently in the future. If you bought stock in a company you didn't truly understand, for example, vow not to do that again.

11

Embrace Feminine Influences

We learned in chapter 2 about the scientific studies showing the differences in the way women and men approach investing, and we discovered that there are even differences attributable to testosterone, or the relative lack thereof. This lack of testosterone tends to make women less willing to take extreme risks, while the herd behavior of testosterone-laden men can possibly make drops in the stock market even more pronounced.

It may seem a stretch to claim Buffett has the testosterone levels of a woman and not a man (remember the "oversexed guy in a harem" comment?). And, well, as much as breaking the news that Buffett's actually a woman might be fun, we've got to admit he is, in fact, a man complete with, yes, testosterone. (And, we're certainly not going to go about the various possible ways to verify this, that's for sure.) However, it is true that he's surrounded himself with a cadre of smart, strong women over the years. Perhaps the influence of those women has resulted in his feminine side shining forth, as we've seen. Let's get acquainted with some of the most important ones.

The late Susan Buffett (known as Susie to her family and friends) was his first wife and one of the biggest influences on

Buffett's adult years. They met when Buffett was a young man, and she was there for the beginning of all that would become legend—Buffett's early job with his idol Ben Graham in New York, his return to his beloved hometown of Omaha, the start of the partnership, the purchase and subsequent transformation of Berkshire Hathaway, and the rise of her husband to the ranks of the rich and powerful.

Through it all, Susie was his protector and tireless supporter. She made it so that he could focus on what he wanted to, as much as he wanted to. Not surprisingly, for Buffett that meant studying annual reports and reading up in his study every night, while Susie looked after their three children. Buffett depended on her, and she's undoubtedly a big part of the reason he was able to become the man he is today. Sadly, she passed away in 2004 of a stroke following a bout with cancer.

Journalist Carol Loomis and bridge champion Sharon Osberg are both close to Buffett, for very different reasons. Loomis has been a longtime friend of his, since meeting him in the 1960s, when she was an investing columnist for *Fortune* (she remains associated with *Fortune* today, as an editor-at-large). Buffett's referred to Loomis as his "best friend," other than Charlie Munger, of course.[1]

Buffett and Loomis hit it off and became fast friends. And we have Loomis to thank, in part, for the clarity and wit Buffett has demonstrated over the years in his letters to shareholders. The earliest letters he wrote had been more like bare-bones financial reporting and much less like the expansive, expressive, folksy letters we enjoy today. In 1978, though, Buffett decided he wanted to start using the letters to educate his partners on the important business issues of the day, as well as teach them timeless investing lessons.

Buffett tapped Loomis for the job of helping him edit each year's offering, and the letters remain today an incredibly useful resource for anyone wanting to learn about investing from the man himself. His voice, temperament, and homespun wisdom shine through in each and every one. In which other giant publicly traded insurance-based holding company's annual letter to shareholders are you going to be graced with quotes from the likes of Mae West, Woody Allen, and just about everyone in between? Which other executives will take the time to teach you, and will be humble enough to admit their mistakes year after year, in clear language? Just one, folks—Buffett. If you haven't yet taken the time to read his shareholder letters, make the time for it. You will not be disappointed. (After you finish this book first, of course!)

Bridge champion Sharon Osberg met Buffett through Carol Loomis in 1993 at a bridge tournament and became another close friend of his, as well as one of his favorite bridge partners. (In addition to his voracious reading, one of Buffett's other loves in life is the card game bridge.) Through playing with Osberg, Buffett's game improved, and his adoration of the game, and of her, deepened. Her relationship with Buffett has blossomed well beyond the card game, and she is a trusted friend and ally, a loyal member of his tight-knit group of friends. Osberg has said of him, "Warren Buffett is my best friend. We talk every day."[2] A December 2009 profile of Buffett and Osberg again confirmed that they remain close, talking several times a day, often while playing bridge online.[3]

Buffett met Katharine Graham, the widowed owner of the Washington Post Company, in 1973, when he first became interested in investing in it. Graham was in charge of running the business following her husband's death, and she was tentative initially about Buffett's intentions. She did not come from a business background and was nervous about losing the business, or just generally about making mistakes while she was in charge.

Buffett had not a bone of ill will in his body, though, and set about teaching Graham about business and finances, helping her learn and showing her that she had the ability and self-confidence to do a great job and be an effective leader. Remember, too, his childhood paper route, delivering the *Washington Post* in the D.C. area while his father was in Congress. He'd long loved the company, and had nothing but admiration for it, and for Graham. They became dear friends and were close until her death in 2001.

In Graham's Pulitzer Prize–winning autobiography, *Personal History*, she writes of Buffett's influence on her in the early days of her leadership at the Post: "My business education began in earnest—he literally took me to business school, which was just what I needed. How lucky I was to be educated—to the extent possible—by Warren Buffett, and how many people would have given anything for the same experience. It was hard work for both of us—Warren admitted I needed what he called 'a little remedial work'—but absolutely vital for me."[4]

For all those years, since 1973, Berkshire's owned a chunk of the Washington Post (about 20 percent at last glance), currently making Buffett's company the largest shareholder of the venerable newspaper and media outfit. Buffett also served since 1974 on the Post's board of directors (minus an eight-year period when he was serving on Capital Cities' board), marking decades of service to the organization. The Post announced in January 2011 that Buffett would be retiring from the board and would not be not seeking reelection for his seat when his term expired in May 2011.[5] He has acknowledged in recent times that the newspaper business is difficult in this current age of readily available free online content, saying he wouldn't invest in another one, but his devotion to the Post and to the Graham family are steadfast.[6] His retirement from the Post's board should not be read as his loyalty wavering, but as a move to simplify his life and focus exclusively on running Berkshire Hathaway. In fact, in classic Buffett form, he said (at the time of the announcement) of Berkshire's investment in the Washington Post Company, "We're going to keep every share of stock we have. I would never sell a share of the Post."[7]

Another woman who influenced Buffett tremendously was entrepreneur Rose Blumkin, a diminutive Russian immigrant who arrived in America at twenty-three in 1917 speaking no English and having no formal education of any sort (we aren't talking no college education here—we are talking no education of *any kind*, ever, period, full stop). Despite what looked like long odds, she started and ran the Nebraska Furniture Mart in Omaha, building an empire from $500.[8]

With an innate business sense, and a focus on value and never spending even a cent more than she had to, Mrs. B, as she was known to everyone in Omaha and eventually to every Berkshire Hathaway shareholder, endeared herself to Buffett. When he talks about Mrs. B in the Berkshire shareholder letters, it's much like the lowly pupil or disciple respecting the master. You can tell that his admiration and respect for her are simply immense. He speaks frequently of her hard work and dedication, saying year after year that she was in the store "seven days a week, from opening to close."[9] And this was when she was in her nineties! Imagine how she must have been for the decades and decades prior to that. It's easy to see why Buffett was inspired by her, and it's impossible not to be inspired ourselves.

In 1983, he bought her business without ever demanding an audit or insisting on seeing an inventory count. This may seem counterintuitive, given that we know Buffett researches so deeply, but it in fact reflects the respect he had for Mrs. B. He just trusted her word, plain and simple; she had that much integrity. She was also a fiery personality and fierce competitor, with the motto "Sell cheap and tell the truth." Mrs. B worked well past the age when most of us would consider retiring because, like Buffett, she truly loved and was obsessed with running her business. She died at age 104 in 1998.

Two current female business leaders Buffett has recently shared his admiration for (choosing, as he often does, the Berkshire shareholder letter as his vehicle for lavishing praise) are Susan Jacques of Borsheim's and Cathy Baron Tamraz of Business Wire, both subsidiaries of Berkshire Hathaway. Of Jacques, Buffett said, "Susan came to Borsheim's 25 years ago as a $4-an-hour saleswoman. Though she lacked a managerial background, I did not hesitate to make her CEO in 1994. She's smart, she loves the business, and she loves her associates. That beats having an MBA degree any time." [10]

He followed up with his thoughts on Tamraz, saying, "Another of our great managers is Cathy Baron Tamraz, who has significantly increased Business Wire's earnings since we purchased it early in 2006. She is an owner's dream. Cathy, it should be noted, began her career as a cab driver." [11]

All of these women's influence on Buffett is as varied as their roles in his life. He appreciates and respects them, though, whether it's for their business sense, their journalistic acumen, their competitive spirit at the bridge table and on the floor of the furniture store, or their loving and giving nature. We can't say for certain that Buffett would not be the investor he is today without knowing and having relationships with them, but it is a safe bet that he's a happier man for it.

While readers of this book, both male and female, probably don't have the benefit of knowing these women as Buffett has, we can still learn from their examples as well. Who doesn't read about Mrs. B and marvel at her ability to overcome obstacles, work hard, and build a store—and a legacy—that endures? Or think how impressive it is that Katharine Graham, going into a difficult and uncertain situation without the knowledge she needed, started from the ground up to learn about business, and eventually grew into a mighty figure in the publishing world? Anyone who's read Buffett's shareholder letters must be grateful to Carol Loomis for helping him find, define, and tweak his remarkable and unique voice over the years. These were influences for Buffett—and vice versa, naturally—but we can, and should, also embrace their stories, appreciating what they've meant to him over the years.

12

Maintain Consistent, Persistent Results

This isn't a trait of female investors and their temperaments, but it's an important outcome, and one we'd be remiss not to talk about. After all, without something to show for all that discipline and calm focus, what's the point, right?

Warren Buffett's been investing since he was a mere eleven years old and managing money professionally on his own since 1956 (when he was just twenty-five years old). During the time we can most easily track his results (that would be the Buffett partnership and Berkshire Hathaway), he's put together an impressive record, one untouchable by anyone else over that length of time. During the years Buffett was running the partnership, from 1956 to 1969, he racked up an astounding 32 percent average annual return before fees. That means for every $10,000 some lucky and/or prescient person invested with Buffett at the beginning of that period, he or she had roughly $300,000 when he closed the partnership down.[1]

Looking at what he's done with Berkshire, the compounded annual gain in per-share book value from 1965 to 2010 is 20.2 percent. Um, not too shabby. That's forty-four years of evidence, forty-four years that Buffett's been success-ful, through recessions and heedless moments of market eu-phoria, through wars, through nine U.S. presidents, through disco, punk rock, new wave, hair metal, grunge, boy bands, and all flavors of hip-hop, through bell-bottoms and platforms the first, second, and third times around, through Fonzie, J. R. Ewing, ALF, the Fresh Prince, and countless ridiculous reality "stars."

Had you instead chosen to just invest your money in an index fund tracking the S&P 500, your average return would have been 9.4 percent, or less than half of Buffett's average year. The overall gain for Berkshire's book value from 1964 to 2009 is 490,409 percent compared to the S&P's 6,262 percent. No, that's not a typo. It really is 490,409 percent.

Given how remarkably good Buffett has been at allocat-ing capital for more than forty years, it's tough to argue that he's been anything *but* consistent and persistent, that he's able to do something special. And yet, beginning in the 1970s and continuing into the 1980s (and even today), that's precisely what some academics tried to argue, dogmatically teaching that Buffett is a mere anomaly, and that the market can't be beaten. The prevailing theory at the time, bouncing along the halls of business schools near and far, is known as the "effi-cient market theory." Without getting too professorial about things (although the tweed coat and leather elbow patches can certainly be adorable): The theory holds that the market fully prices in all available information. That, in turn, means that a stock's full value is always reflected in its price, and therefore there is no such thing as a bargain, or an underpriced or mis-priced security.

That also suggests, on the flip side, that supposed market "bubbles" really aren't. If information is always perfect and prices are always right, that means that shares of Internet company Yahoo!, for instance, trading at a split-adjusted high of $108.17 in the final week of 1999 (compared to the mid-teens both one year *and* ten years later), was appropriate and rational. Um, OK.

So, then, the years that Buffett, and Graham before him, spent searching for companies selling at a reasonable margin of safety were just futile efforts, according to the believers of the efficient market theory. How silly for them to think that the market—which is, don't forget, driven by humans and all their various emotions, along with some giant supercomputers programmed and controlled by humans—could ever be wrong, could ever overreact. In fact, you might as well just throw darts at a page from the *Wall Street Journal* tacked up on your wall than waste another moment analyzing a company. The market had no inefficiencies, so there was no point in trying to discover and exploit them.

But what of the fact that Buffett had produced years upon years of market-beating returns, that he obviously knew how to find companies that were undervalued, that he'd implemented a logical system for finding them, and that he was so darn successful? Oh him. He's just a fluke, the academics argued. He's lucky. Nothing to see here . . . move along.

Buffett took great joy during that time in refuting the EMT theorists. He gave a legendary speech in 1984 at his business school alma mater Columbia, wherein he skewered the efficient market theory proponents by providing example after example of successful investors who'd built strong track records using a Ben Graham and David Dodd–like approach to analyzing companies. Naturally, he included himself in this number, dubbing them all "The Superinvestors of Graham-and-Doddsville."[2]

In the speech, which was reprinted in *Hermes*, the magazine for Columbia's business school, he said, "I'm convinced there is much inefficiency in the market. These Graham-and-Doddsville investors have successfully exploited gaps between price and value. When the price of a stock can be influenced by a 'herd' on Wall Street with prices set at the margin by the most emotional person, or the greediest person, or the most depressed person, it is hard to argue that the market always prices rationally. In fact, the market prices are frequently nonsensical."[3]

The efficient market debate continues, although the growing field of behavioral finance is undermining the theory's validity bit by bit by showing that many times (or perhaps most times), market actions aren't driven by rational people making rational decisions. It is safe to say, though, that the market is, in fact, more efficient than it was when Buffett started out. It's not perfectly efficient, but it's closer, thanks to two complementary factors. First, the sheer availability of information online today makes it much, much easier for small investors to dig through financial statements from their own studies and home offices, hunting for undervalued companies. And the popularity of someone like Buffett means that more investors, young and old, are learning about his methods and putting them into play in the markets. So you've got all these folks looking for similar types of stocks and situations, using lots of the same readily available information.

There will continue to be mispriced stocks, and there will

be superior money managers and investors like Buffett; it's just going to take a little bit more effort to get there. Luckily for the Graham-and-Doddsville investors of the future, there's also no shortage of "smart" people on Wall Street finding the next new "surefire" way to invest, telling the rest of us that "it's different this time." Buffett has also pointed out the upside of teaching efficient market theory to so many students, saying in his 1988 letter to Berkshire shareholders, "In any sort of contest— financial, mental, or physical—it's an enormous advantage to have opponents who have been taught that it's useless to even try. From a selfish point of view, Grahamites should probably endow chairs to ensure the perpetual teaching of EMT."[4]

Now, we know Buffett's performed well, logging incredible gains over his career, but it's also interesting to note that Berkshire Hathaway has, during times of market declines, performed better than the S&P 500. That is, its shares haven't fallen as much, percentagewise, as the S&P did during those periods. This quality makes Berkshire's results even more compelling.

Buffett pointed this out in his 2009 letter to shareholders, writing, "we have never had *any* five-year period beginning with 1965–69 and ending with 2005–09—and there have been 41 of these—during which our gain in book value did not exceed the S&P's gain. Second, though we have lagged the S&P in some years that were positive for the market, we have consistently done better than the S&P in the eleven years during which it delivered negative results. In other words, our defense has been better than our offense, and that's likely to continue."[5]

So, keep the following facts in mind when thinking about performance:

- Ignore anyone who tells you throwing darts at a newspaper is the same as intelligent analysis.
- A good defense is just as valuable as a good offense.
- Stick to a system that's logical and works, and you, too, could build a lengthy and impressive track record.

13

Value People and Relationships

Buffett exemplifies the eight traits we gleaned from the research about female versus male investors exceptionally well, and he certainly is a shining example of market-beating performance. But we can't sum him up that easily. We've got to add three additional principles to fully understand what makes Buffett *Buffett*, what makes him tick, what makes him special, and what makes him the master investor he is. After all, if we are to become better investors ourselves, and that's certainly the goal here, we need to know everything we can about what makes Buffett do the things he does and act the way he acts.

Our first Buffett-centric principle, then, is to value and cultivate your relationships with people. This is something Buffett considers vital to good business. Building lasting relationships with the people you are working with, or investing your money with, or going into business with, is important for long-term success. Buffett places a premium on people, even sometimes putting them ahead of the potential for more profit, and he speaks proudly of this fact.

In a letter to his partners way back in 1968, Buffett said,

"When I am dealing with people I like in businesses I find stimulating (what business isn't?), and achieving worthwhile overall returns on capital employed (say, ten to twelve percent), it seems foolish to rush from situation to situation to earn a few more percentage points. It also does not seem sensible to me to trade known pleasant personal relationships with high-grade people, at a decent rate of return, for possible irritation, aggravation, or worse at potentially higher returns."[1]

And in his 1989 Berkshire letter to shareholders, Buffett echoed this thought, saying, "We have found splendid business relationships to be so rare and so enjoyable that we want to retain all we develop. This decision is particularly easy for us because we feel that these relationships will produce good—though perhaps not optimal—financial results. Considering that, we think it makes little sense for us to give up time with people we know to be interesting and admirable for time with others we do not know and who are likely to have human qualities far closer to average."[2]

Given that we know Buffett is concerned with allocating his capital the most efficient way he can, the fact that he places a high enough value on his relationships to forgo the potential for higher-profit endeavors in favor of continuing to work with people he knows, likes, and trusts shows us how meaningful this is to him. Now, granted, he undoubtedly hopes and wishes that this trade-off won't be necessary, and he'll ideally find situations where he's both making as much money as he possibly can *and* likes the folks he's doing it with. And in fact, Buffett's been adept at finding this mix over his long career.

Speaking of Buffett's focus on the "people" side of investing, Nell Minow, editor and cofounder of The Corporate Library, an organization that focuses on corporate governance, said, "I think one of the most impressive things about him is not the way he looks at stocks, although gosh knows he is very good at math, but the way he looks at people. He has been an excellent judge of people all the way along."[3]

Look at someone like Rose Blumkin, whom we talked about earlier. She was as dedicated to running Nebraska Furniture Mart as Buffett is to investing. He admired her and counted her among the greatest business minds he'd ever known. He knew he didn't need to help Mrs. B run her store; she knew quite well what to do. In turn, she kept working hard for him, growing her business as if she'd never sold it in the first place. And that's exactly as Buffett wants it.

When Buffett buys a company for Berkshire, unlike many other acquirers, he doesn't run right in and start implementing new rules, changing management, and generally stirring up trouble. He buys a company when he believes in the existing management and with the current way a company's being run—otherwise, he'd look elsewhere for opportunities. Buffett does as little as possible to upset the status quo, leaving the management team alone to keep doing what they're doing. He provides guidance and support as needed, but he mostly just stays out of the way.

He feels comfortable operating this way because of the value he places on working with good, smart, motivated people. It makes it easier to sleep at night when you trust the people you're in business with, whether that means buying an entire company outright, or investing in shares of one. For Buffett, quite simply, people matter.

Writing in the Berkshire "Owner's Manual," Buffett says of the managers of Berkshire's subsidiary businesses, "Most of our managers are independently wealthy, and it's therefore up to us to create a climate that encourages them to choose working with Berkshire over golfing or fishing. This leaves us needing to treat them fairly and in the manner that we would wish to be treated if our positions were reversed."[4]

For us, we may not be thinking about buying whole businesses outright (yet), but the people factor still is important. Knowing who's in charge of a company you're thinking about buying shares of is every bit as crucial as it is when Buffett gets to know the people running a business he wants to own.

Now, obviously, it's a little bit easier for Buffett to get face time with those people than it would be for us to, say, call a meeting with the folks in charge of Coca-Cola. But you can still do research and learn as much as you can about just who it is you're entrusting with your money. And that *is* the best way to think about it. It helps keep the importance of having solid, trustworthy management front and center.

KEYS TO ASSESSING MANAGEMENT

In an email interview, Prem Jain, professor at the Georgetown University McDonough School of Business and author of *Buffett Beyond Value: Why Buffett Looks to Growth and Management When Investing*, offers the following suggestions for individual investors trying to assess the quality of management on their own:

"Evaluating company management or a CEO is not easy because different individual qualities can engender success in different circumstances. But I can certainly tell you two fundamental questions to ask. First, are the management team and the current CEO competent? Second, are management incentives properly aligned with shareholder interests?

"To answer the first question, I review the company's performance over several years. For example, when I evaluated Johnson & Johnson and its management, I examined the company's earnings, the return on equity, and the allocation of cash flows for more than 25 years. I prefer evaluating a company's performance over a long period to discover whether management teams can deliver positive results under different CEOs. While it is important to evaluate several metrics, a carefully computed return on equity ratio is probably the most important metric for determining management competence. I found consistently good performance over the entire period, and I did not spot any incongruent acquisitions, large equity issuances, or egregious ethical violations. To me, the results reflected disciplined management. I also read all of the CEO William Weldon's letters to shareholders since he was appointed in 2002.

"To answer the second question, I check the number of shares held by the CEO and other top managers in the company. I am suspicious of CEOs who are awarded a large number of stock options but hold only a small number of shares. In addition, I prefer CEOs who have been with the company for a long time and are promoted from within. They should at the very least have experience in the same industry. Finally, I try to learn about their lifestyle. A CEO with an extravagant lifestyle is less likely to be prudent with shareholders' money than a CEO who lives more modestly.

"Since there is no exact science to evaluating management teams or CEOs, it is important to give yourself a lot of practice. To develop your evaluation skills, I recommend finding several inarguably good CEOs and studying them and their companies. Beyond Warren Buffett, I have benefited from reading articles about and written by Alfred Sloan, Jack Welch, Sam Walton, Jim Sinegal, and several others. An investor can evaluate a CEO or the management team properly only if he or she has first studied many CEOs and management regimes that are known to be successful. The good news is that because there is considerable amount of art in evaluating management, the evaluator gets better with time."[5]

It's easy to find out the names of the top executives at a company you're considering investing in. From there, be like Buffett and read all you can about them. If the company has a website, check it out to see if there are bios available for the top brass. Google the names to see what you can come up with. Read interviews with them if you can find any, or articles written about them or the company. Fool.com is a good place to start. You're looking to find out how long they've been with the company, what their history there is, how much stock of the company they're running they own, and just generally whether you can get a feel for what type of person's in charge.

The desired qualities in management are the same ones we see personified in Buffett—honesty, humility, a passion for business, loyalty, a sense of fairness, an ownership-minded outlook, and even a sense of humor, if you can get it. Someone like Jim Sinegal (whom Prem Jain also singled out; see the sidebar), Costco's cofounder and chief executive officer, is a perfect example. Buffett's owned shares of warehouse retailer Costco for Berkshire, and it's easy to see why. Not only is the business strong, but it's smartly run by a guy who's cut from the same mold that Buffett is.

Sinegal has no pretense about him. He speaks clearly about his business to shareholders and the media alike. He's humble and even answers his own phone—this at a company with a market cap north of $25 billion. (Yes, he really does answer it! But leave the man alone. He's got a business to run, for Pete's sake.) He's passionate about Costco and its employees, too, meaning that people also matter to him as they do to Buffett. He's committed to treating his employees better than average, providing them health insurance, and paying them above-market wages. He believes that all the involved constituencies in a business—shareholders, employees, and customers alike—can win.

You wouldn't even have to know that Berkshire owned shares of Costco to figure any of this out. Just reading interviews with Sinegal and learning about the man himself would show you that he's someone you can believe in and trust with your money. He's never cagey, and Costco doesn't play any accounting shenanigans. Every single tube in that hundred-pack of Aquafresh is accounted for and noted. It's a straightforward company run by a similarly straightforward guy.

HOW THE PROS JUDGE MANAGEMENT

Value investors Lisa Rapuano, of Lane Five Capital Management, and Amelia Weir, of Paradigm Capital Management, also believe that having quality management in place when they invest in a company is key to success. And they sympathize with the plight of small investors trying to figure out if the people running a business are for real or not.

Rapuano says, "I've found that just because somebody's a really smart guy or girl, that doesn't mean they're a great manager of a company. So what I'm assessing on that side is almost always just whether they are very good at capital allocation. That's not just whether or not you buy back stock or what kind of debt you use. That's also what R&D you fund, how you choose to grow, do you understand earning excess returns in your business, and do you understand when it's appropriate not to invest. So I judge the quality of management almost exclusively on whether they get that capital allocation piece of the pie.

"For an average investor, they can do the mathematical thing that I do, which is look at their history of capital allocation. That's something that anyone can do, because you just need the 10-Ks to do that. But the objective judgment of a management team is much tougher. You can't really tell from seeing a guy on CNBC if you can trust him or not.

"You can learn a lot from the conference calls, though. You can learn a lot from how they answer the questions, whether they answer them straightforwardly and how they frame their answers, whether they're aggressive or conciliatory. But you are a little bit out of luck, as an individual, not having access necessarily to them. And frankly, even as a small firm, I don't always have access to CEOs and CFOs. I usually have to win my way into their hearts by proving that I've done all the work, and that often takes a long period of time. Eventually I get in. Sometimes it takes a lot of phone calls, though, asking questions that the IR [investor relations] person can't answer, to demonstrate my interest and my integrity and the work that we've done before finally getting the CEO or the CFO to pay attention."[6]

Weir also thinks the conference calls are a source of good information for individual investors, saying, "To your point about individual investors, if it is a company that I either don't know well or don't feel like I really have my arms around, and this is something that I think does matter for the random person on the street who wants to invest, you can listen to the replay of the conference call or you can read the transcript. I always find it much more useful to listen to the conference call. Because a transcript is a transcript, if you are just looking for some numbers or clarification, but you kind of want to hear what the tone is in management's voice. You want to hear them during the Q&A period. Sometimes some of the analysts are more aggressive or not, but you want to hear what that dialogue is like and are they defensive or are they a little vague or are they really helpful? I think that none of that is an exact science, but I think again, it lends additional information if you are willing to go through that effort to listen to it."[7]

In addition to placing importance on the people he does business with, whether he's buying their company or investing in it, Buffett has also maintained close relationships with certain people for years. He is steadfastly loyal to those close to him. Charlie Munger, who serves as Berkshire's vice chairman and Buffett's right-hand man, is the first and primary person who comes to mind. He is as close to Buffett as anyone has likely ever been and is likely ever to get.

Buffett and Munger (who, as it happens, was also raised in Omaha and even worked in Buffett's grandfather's grocery store as a teenager) met in 1959, and from the beginning, this was a friendship destined to endure.[8] A pair of brainy bookworms, they were both interested in investing and quickly fell into talking for hours on the phone (Munger was living in California, while Buffett was, of course, in Nebraska) and seeing each other in person when they could.[9]

Before long, Buffett and Munger were investing together, doing deals in concert, starting with the aforementioned Hochschild-Kohn investment in 1966. From there they (thankfully) moved on to other, more successful ventures, until they finally combined forces officially. In 1982 Munger became vice chairman of Berkshire Hathaway.[10] Trying to imagine Buffett without Munger is like trying to imagine any famous duo throughout time without both partners. It's Lewis without Clark. Captain without Tennille. Hansel without Gretel. Chocolate without peanut butter.

In other words, Buffett with no Munger would mean a very different future and scenario for both men today. It isn't only that they're pals, either. Munger has had a tremendous influence on Buffett, helping the way he thinks about investing evolve beyond the strict Grahamian cigar butt school of thought. We'll get further into Munger's influence on Buffett in our next chapter.

Another person whom Buffett counts as a close friend might surprise you, given Buffett's public aversion to technology—that's Bill Gates, cofounder of computer software giant Microsoft. The two, who have since volleyed back and forth in rankings on the *Forbes* list of richest people in the world, met in 1991. They formed a quick friendship, built on mutual respect and appreciation for one another. Buffett got Gates to take up his favorite pastime, bridge, and even helped out when Gates was asking for his wife's hand in marriage. (Buffett and Gates tricked Melinda, his betrothed, into coming to Omaha and then opened up Borsheim's, a local jewelry store Berkshire Hathaway owns, for her to choose her engagement ring.)[11]

Though it began as a friendship, it has grown into a business relationship, with Buffett asking Gates to serve on the board of directors of Berkshire in 2004. In June 2006 Buffett announced that he would be donating 85 percent of his Berkshire Hathaway stock over time to charitable organizations, with the bulk of that going to the Bill & Melinda Gates Foundation.[12] More recently, Buffett and Gates have started a campaign together to encourage other billionaires to donate half their money to charity.[13]

Buffett is loyal to his inner circle of friends, choosing to work with and interact with the same core group for years. In addition to Munger and Gates, he's tight with Tom Murphy, who was in charge of Capital Cities, the company that eventually bought the television network ABC, and then would sell to Disney. Berkshire owned shares of ABC at the time it was sold, and Buffett actually counts *not* investing in an earlier TV deal that Murphy was selling him on as one of his biggest mistakes of omission.

Through the years he was also close friends with the late Bill Ruane, a talented fund manager Buffett met at Columbia. It was actually Ruane's newly formed Sequoia fund that Buffett suggested his partners invest in when he shut down his partnership in 1969.[14] Buffett met Walter Schloss, another giant of the value investing world, at the first annual meeting he ever attended, while he was at Columbia.[15] Buffett featured both Ruane and Schloss, along with Munger, in his "Graham and Doddsville" speech at Columbia as examples of investors like himself whose long track records of success at picking stocks made the efficient market theory look like hogwash.

Buffett realizes that the people you choose to do business with and associate with can have a huge effect on your outcome. He also knows that good businesses do better with good people in charge, people you can trust to behave ethically and honestly. The most perfect business in the world, with a large, well-protected moat, ample cash flows, and a fat margin of safety won't compel him to invest unless the people portion of the equation is just as strong. And once he's committed to a business with management he likes, he is loyal and sticks by them.

Writing in his 1986 letter to shareholders, Buffett said, "We intend to continue our practice of working only with people whom we like and admire. This policy not only maximized our chances for good results, it also ensures us an extraordinarily good time. On the other hand, working with people who cause your stomach to churn seems much like marrying for money—probably a bad idea under any circumstances, but absolute madness if you are already rich."[16]

For us, this is something we can also put into play in our investing lives, and we should. Keep the following in mind:

- A business is only as strong as the people running it.
- Read up on the management of companies you are considering investing in. Look for smart, open, loyal, fair executives you can admire.
- Don't be afraid to put people before profit; Buffett isn't.

14

Question the Masters

Not everyone is lucky enough to study under a certified guru, and their eventual mentor, in graduate school, but Warren Buffett did just that when he went to Columbia, home to Ben Graham and David Dodd, the powerful twosome who'd literally written the book on value investing. Buffett was quickly thrust into a world that was heaven to him. Analyzing companies, reading everything he could get his hands on, and having the chance to sit in classrooms and have discussions and debates with Graham was like coming home for Buffett.

He soaked up everything he could while he was there, and made connections with Graham and other like-minded students that would carry on long past the closing school bell. From Graham, he built the core of his investing philosophy: Always buy with a margin of safety. As we talked about earlier, in the chapter on risk, Buffett considers these three words— "margin of safety"—to be the "cornerstone of successful investing."[1]

Buffett also learned the basics of value investing from Graham. He learned about calculating intrinsic value, figuring out how much a company was currently worth, and how much it should be worth in the future. He learned about the vagaries of the market, especially the character Graham loved to talk about, Mr. Market, and all his associated capriciousness.

Buffett, it's safe to say, idolized Ben Graham and most likely continues to idolize him to this very day. Buffett wouldn't have become the investor he is today without Graham's foundation.

And yet, Buffett, as he began his investing career and started learning more about business and what makes companies successful, slowly started shifting his orientation. He was still solidly in the value camp (although he's actually argued in his shareholder letters that the value-versus-growth distinction is a meaningless one, as you need both in order for a company to turn into a winning investment), but he began looking at more qualitative factors, as opposed to the strictly quantitative ones Graham focused on.

You see, for Graham, it was all about the numbers. It didn't even matter much what the company did, or who was on its executive team, or what its future prospects held. While he firmly believed in the fact that buying a stock was buying a piece of an actual, living and breathing company, he was also more concerned with tallying up a company's assets and liabilities and seeing what the whole shebang was worth, and then seeing what it was trading for in the market.

This was the "cigar butt" school of investing we covered earlier. The goal was to stumble across a cigar that had just *one* more puff in it, and take advantage of that. Buffett, however, was destined to become something more than a mere cigar butt aficionado. He was to see that just because something's exceedingly cheap, that doesn't by default make it good.

The first person to open Buffett's eyes to this was Charlie Munger. Munger took more nebulous factors into consideration when he invested. While he also didn't like overpaying for businesses, the fact that something was cheaper than dirt was not the be-all and end-all for him. That in and of itself was not enough of a reason to buy.

He believed that management mattered, that having a competitive advantage mattered, and that sometimes you had to pay a little bit more than you would have liked to own a piece of a promising business. Instead of hunting around for nasty old cigar butts to suck one last puff from, Munger's philosophy was, essentially, "Why don't we look for great businesses run by good folks and buy those?"[2]

For Buffett, this was something of a revelation. He slowly began to see that Munger was right, and that he could take the best of Graham and add in some more qualitative factors to come up with a comprehensive investing philosophy that was his own.

The work of investment writer Philip Fisher was also important here. Fisher wrote a highly influential book, *Common Stocks and Uncommon Profits*, where he laid out his approach to investing. This involved something he dubbed "scuttlebutt," which meant the research into a company's prospects an investor could engage in on his own.[3] It could mean talking to management, or a company's suppliers, or its customers, or its employees, or just generally being alert to picking up new information.

This fit beautifully with Buffett's feelings that research

was something you never got enough of. And he'd already engaged in scuttlebutt himself by that point. Showing up as a grad student at GEICO's offices on a Saturday and talking to a vice president jumps right to mind. (Scuttlebutt's something you can do, too. It's an excellent way to learn more about your investments.)

In addition to giving the world *scuttlebutt* (which, incidentally, is also the name of a "gentlemen's club" in Slidell, Louisiana), Fisher's investing masterpiece also focused, in large part, on the more qualitative factors Buffett was picking up from Munger. Fisher's book provided a fifteen-point list of things to look for when analyzing a company. Among them were several points devoted to the importance of having open, honest management, as well as questions about the strength of the company's product line and its viability versus its competitors.

By 1989, Buffett had fully turned the philosophical corner and in his letter to shareholders that year said, "A cigar butt found on the street that has only one puff left in it may not offer much of a smoke, but the 'bargain purchase' will make that puff all profit. Unless you are a liquidator, that kind of approach to buying businesses is foolish."[4]

He went on to talk about his experience with the Baltimore department store he and Munger bought, Hochschild-Kohn, which gave them such fits. It was cheap as cheap could be when he bought it. It even had good people running it. But those fine folks weren't enough to overcome plain old bad economics. As an example of why pure cigar butt investing didn't work, that was a good one.

Buffett also differed from Graham on the issue of diversification. Graham owned lots and lots of companies, while

Buffett believes in focusing on just a few. He believes that owning lots of stocks is a sign that you don't fully understand what you're doing, while Graham believed (as do we here at The Motley Fool) that it reduces your risk.

Writing in the 1993 letter to Berkshire shareholders, Buffett addressed this point, saying, "Charlie and I decided long ago that in an investment lifetime it's too hard to make hundreds of smart decisions. . . . Therefore we adopted a strategy that required our being smart—and not too smart at that—only a few times. . . . The strategy we've adopted precludes our following standard diversification dogma. Many pundits would therefore say the strategy must be riskier than that employed by more conventional investors. We disagree. We believe that a policy of portfolio concentration may well *decrease* risk if it raises, as it should, both the intensity with which an investor thinks about a business and the comfort-level he must feel with its economic characteristics before buying into it. In stating this opinion, we define risk, using dictionary terms, as 'the possibility of loss or injury.' "[5]

Buffett's investment in GEICO when he was a grad student, and after he went down in person to the company's D.C.-based office (scuttlebutt!), provides a good example of the difference between Graham and Buffett on the issue of diversification. While Graham owned small stakes of many companies, Buffett was such a profound believer in GEICO already that the young student invested three-quarters of his portfolio in it.[6] Concentrating like this in one stock is pure Buffett.

So, while it's important to learn from those who've gone before you, don't be afraid to ask if the way they are going about things is the best way possible. Remember:

- The learning never stops, so even after you think you've figured out the best way to invest, keep studying.
- Just because someone's an acknowledged investment guru or master doesn't mean there isn't a better way.
- You aren't committing blasphemy when you question anybody, Warren Buffett included.

15

Act Fairly and Ethically

Our final Buffett-related principle is something we touched on earlier when we talked about what to look for when evaluating management—and that's finding people who are ethical and fair. Buffett has always conducted himself this way, nearly to a fault, as we'll see, and it's tragic but true that in this day and age that's pretty unusual. However, as Buffett demonstrates, success can, in fact, come to those who play nice. (And that's the way it should be!)

One significant way that Buffett embodies this idea of fairness is his belief that all shareholders, no matter how big their stake or how tiny, deserve to be updated at the same time and in the same manner. This may sound like an obvious tenet, and one not particular to Buffett, but in fact, things on Wall Street weren't always this way. Many companies over the years have given precedence to the large, institutional shareholders of their stock, or to the analysts on the Street following their company, essentially slamming the door in the face of the small individual investor, a now-illegal practice known as "selective disclosure."

In fact, Arthur Levitt, then chairman of the Securities and

Exchange Commission, commended The Motley Fool for our advocacy that this shady practice should be stopped.[1] With the passage of Regulation Fair Disclosure, in August 2000, it finally was. The playing field was, as they say, level at last. Buffett called selective disclosure "corrupt" and said, "The fact that this reform came about because of coercion rather than conscience should be a matter of shame for CEOs and their investor relations departments."[2]

This was never the case with Buffett and Berkshire, however. Buffett believes strongly in not giving advantages to one group of shareholders over another. Everyone should be treated equally and fairly. Writing in the Berkshire "Owner's Manual," Buffett says, "In all of our communications, we try to make sure that no single shareholder gets an edge: We do not follow the usual practice of giving earnings 'guidance' to analysts or large shareholders. Our goal is to have all of our owners updated at the same time."[3]

In addition to making sure everyone gets the same information simultaneously, Buffett also works hard to give his shareholders just as much info on how Berkshire's performing as he would want were he in their shoes. And he does it with clear language and an openness to revealing as much as he feasibly can (without giving anything away to competitors).

Writing again in the Owner's Manual, Buffett says, "We will be candid in our reporting to you, emphasizing the pluses and minuses important in appraising business value. Our guideline is to tell you the business facts that we would want to know if our positions were reversed. We owe you no less. . . . We also believe candor benefits us as managers: The CEO who misleads others in public may eventually mislead himself in private."[4]

Buffett holds the notion that his shareholders are more like family than acquaintances, so communicating effectively with them is a priority for him. When he refers to them as his "partners" in Berkshire Hathaway, he means it. He's not just giving that idea lip service. It goes hand in hand with his strong belief that when you buy shares in a company, you are buying a piece of a business, and you are truly an owner of that business. Remember that and don't allow yourself to be treated as anything less. Demand that all the executive teams running your companies—and they *are* your companies—speak honestly and clearly with you and your fellow shareholders. All investors, big and small, deserve that.

Buffett's found that being fair can raise some eyebrows, with he and Munger once having to defend themselves to the Securities and Exchange Commission for overpaying for a company that they wanted to buy. Yes, you read that right— Buffett and Munger were once investigated for willingly paying *too much* for a company they were trying to purchase in full. Not surprisingly, the firm that Buffett and Munger were trying to buy wasn't the one raising a fuss about how much they wanted to pay. It was another company, which was supposed to merge with their target for a much cheaper price, that called foul on them.

Wesco, which is now a fully owned subsidiary of Berkshire and run by Charlie Munger, is the company in question. Way back in the 1970s, before they'd fully joined forces, Buffett and Munger were investing together using different companies to buy shares of others. Through one of these combo efforts, Blue Chip Stamps, they'd bought some shares of Wesco, which was a California savings and loan firm.

Not long after they started buying shares, Wesco announced

it was merging with another California bank, but Buffett and Munger didn't like or approve of the price. They both believed the company was letting itself go for too little. While they met with and got to know some of the executives at the company, they started buying Wesco shares at above what the stock market was pricing them at. Because the original deal had apparently fallen apart, investors were driving Wesco shares down, and Buffett and Munger did not want to take advantage of this fact, especially since in a sense, they'd caused it. Eventually, they bought the rest of the company, also for above what shares were trading at at the time.

Government investigators were confused as to why two smart and able money managers like Buffett and Munger would willingly do this. Munger's entreaty that it was the "right thing" to do didn't persuade them. It was just unfathomable that investors would decide to pay more than they had to, to acquire a company they wanted. In the end, luckily, Buffett and Munger escaped virtually unscathed from the legal morass. They were able to buy Wesco outright, as they'd wanted all along, at a price that to them represented what was fair.

Earlier in his career, Buffett had also chosen to stand up for what he saw was right and fair. In 1964, a small subsidiary of American Express was involved in a scandal that cost some banks that had loaned it money millions of dollars, but did not ultimately affect the overall strength of the company's brand, main business line, or future prospects. The market sold the stock off, and Buffett, ever the brave soul to step in where others would not, starting buying shares of it for the partnership. Trying to move beyond the scandal, American Express was ponying up money to settle the banks' claims, but some shareholders sued, arguing that instead of paying up, the company should defend itself.

Buffett came out strongly on the side of American Express doing the right thing, which was, as he saw it, making good by paying the banks off. He believed the company would be "worth very substantially more" if it did right by the banks versus fighting them.[5] American Express listened, and it turned out that Buffett was right. The stock recovered more than 40 percent from its lows, and remains a significant Berkshire Hathaway holding today.

One final incident represents Buffett's feelings about the importance of ethics in business. In the early 1990s, a rogue bond trader at Salomon Brothers, the now long-gone Wall Street investment house, created a scandal for the company by engaging in dubious practices when it came to the Treasury bond market. Essentially, he was creating fake accounts to corner the market and buy more than Salomon's fair share of bonds from the government for resale.

Berkshire owned a chunk of Salomon at the time, although Buffett knew nothing about the misdeeds at the company. The top guys in charge resigned, and Buffett was asked to step in and serve as interim chairman. This was a role he did not relish, but he made the tough choice and agreed to do it. He shook Salomon to its core with his open attitudes and willingness to be honest with the media and others.

Buffett agreed, naturally, to cooperate with the government's inquiry into Salomon's doings. And it was his 1991 congressional testimony on the Salomon Brothers scandal that allowed him to express his feelings on the importance of ethics most clearly: "After they first obey all rules, I then want employees to ask themselves whether they are willing to have any contemplated act appear the next day on the front page of their local paper, to be read by their spouses, children and friends, with the reporting done by an informed and critical reporter. If they follow this test, they need not fear my other message to them: Lose money for the firm and I will be understanding. Lose a shred of reputation for the firm and I will be ruthless."[6]

Warren Buffett takes doing the right thing very seriously, and over the long term, the evidence from him bears out that in addition to simply being the most karma-friendly way to go, it also leads to wealth. Doing right by other people, being fair, and having the attitude that everyone can win is a great framework with which to approach investing. It allows you to look for opportunities that can both make you feel good *and* make you rich.

So, remember:

- You can be good and be rich; one doesn't preclude the other.
- It's possible to find companies where employees, shareholders, and customers all win, and those can make for winning investments.
- Look for companies that communicate in an open, honest way. You, as an owner, deserve to be treated this way.

16

Foolish Investing Principles 101

OK, now that you know just about everything there is to know about Warren Buffett and his "feminine" temperament, let's take a minute to recap the lessons we've learned from each of the eight feminine investing traits as well as our three "Buffett-esque" principles. Then we'll talk about how to take all the knowledge we've learned so far and apply it to a Foolish investment philosophy.

Female investors tend to:

1. Trade less than men do
   - Remember you're buying a piece of an actual business.
   - Take the long view.
   - Be patient.

2. Exhibit less overconfidence: men think they know more than they do, while women are more likely to know what they don't know
   - Buffett's "sphere of understanding" may be different from your own.

- Think about and learn what your own circle of competence covers.
- Stick to it, no matter what.

3. Shun risk more than male investors do
   - Insist on an appropriate margin of safety.
   - Avoid debt as much as possible.
   - Stay within your circle of competence.
   - Do your homework before investing overseas.

4. Be less optimistic, and therefore more realistic, than their male counterparts
   - Be levelheaded about your investments and the market at large. Learn not to be excited by market swings to the upside or devastated by market drops.
   - You're in charge of Mr. Market. Don't let him boss you around.
   - Quoting Buffett, "When investing, pessimism is your friend, euphoria the enemy."

5. Put in more time and effort researching possible investments, considering every angle and detail, as well as considering alternate points of view
   - Read, read, read.
   - Don't forget about your circle of competence.
   - Avoid confirmation bias—seek out information that contradicts your conclusions, not just information that reinforces them.

6. Be more immune to peer pressure and tend to make decisions the same way regardless of who's watching
   - Be willing to be contrarian, as uncomfortable as it may be.

- Take Buffett's words to heart: "Be greedy when others are fearful, and fearful when others are greedy."
- Live by your own Inner Scorecard.

7. Learn from their mistakes
   - You're going to make mistakes. We all do. So don't beat yourself up when you slip up.
   - Assess what happened. Did you miss something? Or did market conditions change?
   - Think about what you can reasonably do differently in the future. If you bought stock in a company you didn't truly understand, for example, vow not to do that again.

8. Thanks to good old biology, have less testosterone than men do, making them lesss willing to take extreme risks, which, in turn, could lead to less extreme market cycles.

While not a trait of the female investing temperament, the outcome of this investing style is important. Therefore, remember that female investors produce results that are more consistent and persistent. And in the hedge fund world, female-managed hedge funds outperform comparable male-managed hedge funds, and they don't suffer from market drops as severely.

- Ignore anyone who tells you throwing darts at a newspaper is the same as intelligent analysis.
- A good defense is just as valuable as a good offense.
- Stick to a system that's logical and works, and you, too, could build a lengthy and impressive track record.

And our three Buffett-centric principles:

1. Value and cultivate your relationships with people
   - A business is only as strong as the people running it.
   - Read up on the management of companies you are considering investing in. Look for smart, open, loyal, fair executives you can admire.
   - Don't be afraid to put people before profit; Buffett isn't.

2. Learn from the masters, but be willing to question them
   - The learning never stops, so even after you think you've figured out the best way to invest, keep studying.
   - Just because someone's an acknowledged investment guru or master doesn't mean there isn't a better way.
   - You aren't committing blasphemy when you question anybody, Warren Buffett included.

3. Be fair and operate in an ethical manner
   - You can be good and be rich; one doesn't preclude the other.
   - It's possible to find companies where employees, shareholders, and customers all win, and those can make for winning investments.
   - Look for companies that communicate in an open, honest way. You, as an owner, deserve to be treated this way.

Now that we've broken down the qualities and temperament that make Warren Buffett the investor he is, and we've discovered the investing traits that female investors tend to share (and use to edge out the boys), what more is there to it? Well, lots actually. The Motley Fool has spent years educating, amusing, and enriching investors all over the world, and while you're already well on your way to being a successful investor, you've still got more to learn. So, let's jump right in. The first few principles will be familiar to you at this point, but they're important enough to touch on again.

- Buy a stock, buy a business.
- Buy what you know.
- Long-term buy-to-hold is the way to go.
- Compound interest is a miraculous thing.
- Save to grow.
- Invest now?
- Get your assets allocated.
- Diversify. Yes, diversify.
- What, me sell?

■ BUY A STOCK, BUY A BUSINESS.

As we learned earlier, when you buy a share of stock, you are investing in an actual business. Keeping this fact in mind helps separate the mere speculators (boo, hiss) from the bona fide investors (wild applause). Consider yourself a business owner, whether you've just ponied up for 100 shares of Hershey or 10,000 shares of Target.

The Motley Fool holds this tenet near and dear, and it's the foundation for our entire investing philosophy, as it is for Buffett. Don't you forget it, either. You aren't just typing in three or four random letters into your online broker's website and then pushing "submit." You are buying a part of a business, just as if you went out and bought the lemonade stand from those cute kids on the corner (can you believe how much they charge for that stuff?).

Key takeaway: You aren't buying something abstract when you invest. You're becoming a business owner.

■ BUY WHAT YOU KNOW.

We also believe, as does Buffett, in staying within your circle of competence. Another famous investment mind, Peter Lynch, who ran the incredibly successful Magellan Fund for Fidelity for years, popularized the phrase "Buy what you know," and that works here, too.

Essentially, you want to be able to understand what you're investing in. It follows behind what we just talked about—if you believe you are buying a piece of an actual business (and you are), then you should be able to explain what that business does, and understand how it makes money. For beginning investors, this often means buying shares of companies that sell products you use or know well. Look around you—there are investment opportunities and possibilities all around.

The danger of going too far afield of what you can reasonably understand raises the chance that you'll invest in something you can't adequately follow and feel comfortable owning over the long term. And that's what this is all about—long-term stock ownership.

Key takeaway: Understand what you're investing in. It lowers your risk when you do so.

■ LONG-TERM BUY-TO-HOLD IS THE WAY TO GO.

Speaking of the long term, this is another facet of Buffett's investing philosophy that we strongly believe in at The Motley

Fool. Buying a stock only to sell it days later, or worse, minutes or hours later, does not interest us. That's a small-*f* foolish way to invest. When you're thinking like a business owner, you are thinking long-term.

Individual investors also have a tremendous advantage when it comes to being able to effectively stay put and avoid trading. Unlike mutual funds or big institutional investors, which are constantly dealing with withdrawals and are therefore often forced to sell in order to generate cash, the little guys and gals like us can, instead, afford to hunker down with our stocks, keeping them near and dear for years on end. Don't let this important advantage pass you by.

Additionally, when you buy and sell more than you should, you rack up trading costs and tax bills. Even supposing you were gifted with an uncanny ability to be a hotshot short-term trader, the bite that those costs would take from your returns would be painful. It's one of the reasons women tend to show better results than men do (since they trade less than men).

We believe in long-term buy-to-hold. That doesn't mean you buy stocks and then never look at them ever again. We aren't suggesting that. But with the proper mindset that you are buying a piece of a business that you will likely own for years, we believe you should instead monitor your investments to keep an eye on them and make sure nothing drastic has changed.

A helpful tip for putting this into practice is to write down all the reasons you bought a stock at the time you bought it. Document, document, document. Think about what factors could lead you to sell, and jot those down, too. It's inevitable that you will sell stocks in your lifetime. Buffett does it;

everyone does it. The important thing is not to do it for the wrong reasons. There will be times when a company's outlook and circumstances change enough that you decide it's time to part with your shares, for example. But it can be difficult to remember what exactly compelled you to buy the company in the first place. If you have a record of your thinking, you have a framework to start from.

Check in on your companies at least quarterly. Read up on how they're doing and assess what's going on with them versus your documented reasons for buying in the first place. Our goal, hope, and wish, like Buffett's, is to hold a stock forever, but that doesn't mean you should completely ignore it once you own it. Your money, your capital, is precious, and it's up to you to ensure that it's invested in the best possible places.

Key takeaway: Don't invest and then never glance your stocks' way again. Keep up with the business performance of them—but don't obsess on the stock price. That's no way to judge a company's progress.

■ COMPOUND INTEREST IS A MIRACULOUS THING.

Another reason to be long-term focused is the amazing power of compound interest. Like kudzu or bacteria, compound interest just keeps growing over time. The concept's not complicated, for something so powerful. When you have money invested and you're earning a rate of return on it (so, say, your stock portfolio goes up 6 percent a year), and then you think about the length of time you have your money earning that, each and every year the amount you have is growing—so the base amount you have for the following year is even greater!

OK, so maybe that is complicated. Let's try a table. Let's assume you started off with $1,200 invested four different ways over a period of years.

	Savings Account (0.5%)	Money Market Fund (2%)	Certificate of Deposit (5%)	Stock Market (9%*)
Initial investment	$1,200	$1,200	$1,200	$ 1,200
5 years	$1,230	$1,325	$1,532	$ 1,846
10 years	$1,261	$1,463	$1,955	$ 2,841
15 years	$1,293	$1,615	$2,495	$ 4,371
20 years	$1,326	$1,783	$3,184	$ 6,725
25 years	$1,359	$1,969	$4,064	$10,348
30 years	$1,394	$2,174	$5,186	$15,921
35 years	$1,429	$2,400	$6,619	$24,497
40 years	$1,465	$2,650	$8,448	$37,691

*Based on the stock market's historical return

Remember, that's $1,200 you did nothing else with. You didn't add any money over the years, and it grew all on its own to $37,691 over 40 years.

(This table brings up another good point—investing in stocks over the long term will bring you a much better return than other vehicles like savings accounts or money market funds. Given that you're reading a book about investing in the stock market, this probably isn't news to you, but it's worth pointing out nonetheless.)

Now let's look at another scenario that demonstrates the power of compound interest. Let's say you start with $1,200 in your first year of saving and then each and every year, you add $1,200 to your original stash. Where do you end up now?

	Savings Account (0.5%)	Money Market Fund (2%)	Certificate of Deposit (5%)	Stock Market (9%)*
Initial Investment	$ 1,200	$ 1,200	$ 1,200	$ 1,200
5 years	$ 6,091	$ 6,370	$ 6,962	$ 7,828
10 years	$12,335	$13,402	$ 15,848	$ 19,872
15 years	$18,737	$21,167	$ 27,189	$ 38,404
20 years	$25,301	$29,740	$ 41,663	$ 66,917
25 years	$32,030	$39,205	$ 60,136	$ 110,789
30 years	$38,930	$49,655	$ 83,713	$178,290
35 years	$46,003	$61,193	$113,804	$282,150
40 years	$53,256	$73,932	$152,208	$441,950

* Based on the stock market's historical return

Wooooo, now that's more like it! And to improve upon that cool $441,950, you could sock away more than $1,200 a year over that period. More than double it to starting with $2,800 a year and adding $2,800 a year and you're looking at a million bucks after 40 years.

Once you come to appreciate the full power of compound interest, you'll see why it's smart to be invested over the long haul. You need time to make compound interest really work for you. The power it has to build and build and build becomes magnified only with time.

Key takeaway: Take advantage of the full power of compound interest by giving your investments time to grow.

■ **SAVE TO GROW.**

In order to have money to invest in stocks, and thus begin benefiting from the joys of compounding interest, you've got to save some up. And if you're carrying around credit card debt, like so many Americans (at last check the average credit card debt per person was nearly $5,000), you're going to need to address that little issue *before* you start investing. Yes, it can hurt, because we know you're itching to become tomorrow's Buffett, but you need to get your financial house in order first.

The reason why is this: The interest rate on your credit card debt is almost certainly higher than the return you could earn in the stock market. You could very well be paying 17 percent interest on your credit card debt while you're trying to earn 9 percent in the stock market, for instance. That makes no sense. (Note: Consider investing in one of those credit card companies, because those folks are raking it in!) And because just to keep your debt at bay you're paying out more in interest each month than you'd be making in the market, you're stagnating or even falling behind overall.

The soundest course of action here is to come up with a plan to pay more than the minimum balance on your debt each and every month until you get rid of that sucker. Then, and only then, should you consider investing in the market. Heck, even if you're not quite ready to invest on your own, paying off your credit card debt is still a worthy endeavor. That interest will eat you alive, making the things you purchased (did you really need that second pair of Uggs? did you even need that first pair?) cost way more than they should have.

Remember what we learned about Buffett—he's not a fan of debt. Listen to him. He knows what he's talking about. Out-of-hand debt can saddle your prosperous financial future, making it so much harder than it has to be.

One final word on savings—once you've got your debt

situation all squared away (yay, you!), set some money aside in a safe place as an "emergency fund." Stuff, as they say, happens, and you want to be ready for it when it does. Broken-down cars, home repairs, last-minute flight and tickets to see U2 in Dublin (ahem) . . . all things that are unanticipated and can be pricey. So save some money and keep it handy, just in case.

Key takeaway: There's some truth to that old saw, "It takes money to make money." Thing is, you need to make sure your money isn't being held hostage by credit card interest rates before you can put it to work for you.

▦ INVEST NOW?

OK, so you've cleared out any credit card debt, saved enough for an emergency fund (oh, Bono), and have come to love, appreciate, and respect your new best friend, compound interest. You're ready, you understand you're buying a piece of an actual business, and you are in this thing for the long haul.

Or are you?

Ask yourself how quickly you're going to need access to the money you have saved up and want to invest. Looking to buy a house in two years and need this cash for a down payment? Don't invest it in the stock market, then. Kid going off to get an Ivy League education (or even a junior-college-in-the-next-town-over education) next fall? Don't invest. Trying to buy the RV of your dreams in a few years? Don't invest.

Sorry to be so negative, but this one's important—only invest money in the stock market when you won't need it for at least five years or more. Remember the nature of Ben Graham's fabled Mr. Market character? He can be depressed for years, then happy for a couple of months, then sad again. He's all over the place, this guy. You do not want any money you need in the short term to be at his mercy. Don't do it.

Over time, the stock market is where it's at, but the key here is that you have to be committed to letting your money be yanked about by Mr. Market in the short term. If you need that money soon, stick it in a savings account or other less risky vehicle somewhere, like a certificate of deposit or money market fund.

Taking the long view, Mr. Market looks less crazy. The bumps and curves and crying fits (he can be so annoying when he's like that) all smooth out, but it takes time. For long periods, the stock market really is the best place to be invested. You just have to be ready and able to take the bad along with the good.

Key takeaway: Don't even think about investing money in the market that you need in less than five years. Seriously, don't even think about it.

JUST STARTING OUT? LISTEN UP!

Here are some sage words of advice for beginning investors, from people who've been there:

"Don't borrow money. Debt is the four-letter word that can undo a lot of good work. Buffett has said only invest in what you understand. Be sure the company has durable competitive advantages and be sure the management is top-notch. Think for yourself."[1]

—Andrew Kilpatrick, author of
Of Permanent Value: The Story of Warren Buffett

"Don't watch CNBC. That's sort of flip, but the real message is, 'You have to find your own strategy.' You can't copy or react to other people. It's a very self-analytical process. Focus on what you do well and what your skill set is and don't worry about what everybody else is doing."[2]

—Lisa Rapuano, founder, Lane Five Capital Management

"As a beginning investor, I would say start where you have some kind of comfort zone, some touchstone that makes you think this makes sense to you. Maybe it is buying shares in the local bank, if you have always done your banking there or buying ten shares of Nike because you like Nike's running shoes and you think it is a good company. Go somewhere where you have some real tangible thought about the company and not, 'So-and-so said to buy this stock because it is going to go up next month.'"[3]

—Candace King Weir, founder, Paradigm Capital Management

"They say that so many guitar players really burn out because they try to emulate Jimi Hendrix and so many drummers burn out because they try to emulate Neil Peart, and I think that there is something to be said about not trying to be someone else. To being true to yourself and not trying to emulate even someone who is as spectacular as Warren Buffett. He can divide complex fractions in his head. He is really a talent without compare. He is kind of an island unto himself.

"I think a lot of people just really try to be the next Buffett instead of trying to be the first whoever they are. Investing is hard enough without saying, 'Well, my instinct says X, but Warren Buffett says Y, so I am going to do Y.' I think that is a very important thing for people who are just starting out.

"My second piece of advice would be to take your time. There is no rush. So many times with beginning investors they get awfully excited about it and before they have studied it for six months, they own 20 different things with 95 percent of their money, and that is scary. It is

■ **GET YOUR ASSETS ALLOCATED.**

All right, so you've rid yourself of credit card debt, you have your emergency cash safely stashed, and the money you're investing is money you don't need access to for five years or more. There's one additional time-based factor you need to consider, and that's what's called your time horizon. Think of it as the time you have stretched out before you to be invested. How much time you have ahead of you determines, in part, how much of your portfolio should be in stocks.

Let's say you're fresh out of college and have your first real "grown-up" job. Aside from getting used to being up early every day and dressing up beyond some patterned PJ pants and an "ironic" *Saved by the Bell* T-shirt, you should also take this opportunity to invest. You have years and years and years of earning potential ahead of you, so make the most of it! You can afford to take more risk than older investors can, which means you should have all of your portfolio (which is likely still humble at this point, but that's cool—remember the power of compounding!) in stocks. You have the time to put up with the market's ups and downs, so start investing early to take advantage of your youth.

Or how about someone in her late 30s or early 40s? She's been working for a good 15–20 years or so, saving and investing along the way. She may have a child or two, so she's socking money away for their future, as well. Should she still be invested in stocks? You bet. She probably wouldn't want to have her entire portfolio in risky high-flying growth stocks (such as those in emerging industries like biotechnology) even if she works in the field and can fully understand them. Balancing them out with some safer, bigger companies makes sense. And it probably also makes sense here to start considering asset classes other than equities to better balance her risk. But she should absolutely still be in stocks.

Someone closer to retirement age, or already retired, should start shifting more of their assets to safer, but slower-growing, assets like bonds. You're going to start needing to count on that money sooner than our fresh-out-of-college kid, so you're going to want it to seek shelter from Mr. Market's mania. Still, we don't believe you should ever be all the way out of stocks. At this point start looking for established dividend-payers. The benefits are twofold: They're less likely to be volatile, and you'll get income from your dividends in retirement.

There's one more important point to think about here, and that involves making sure you can sleep at night. No, we aren't talking about instituting a nightly snack of milk and cookies (mmmm, peanut butter and chocolate chip). Instead, you need to consider how much risk you can tolerate—how much you can stand to see your stocks go down. Be honest about how much psychological distress you would be in if your stocks dropped 10 percent tomorrow, or 20 percent over the next few weeks, or 40 percent next year (as they actually did in 2008).

As we discussed earlier, all investing involves risk, and it's inevitable that you will lose money. You need to be as prepared for that reality as possible. Now, if you are able to keep the freakouts to a minimum and more importantly **don't sell**, you won't lock in those losses, but you have to be able to withstand the pressure.

Author William J. Bernstein, in his book *The Four Pillars of Investing*, provides a useful table for figuring out how much of your portfolio should be in stocks based on how much downside you could tolerate:[5]

I can tolerate losing ____% of my portfolio in the course of earning higher returns	Recommended % of portfolio invested in stocks
35%	80%
30%	70%
25%	60%
20%	50%
15%	40%
10%	30%
5%	20%
0%	10%

So if you can't take losing 20 percent or more of your money, then no more than half of your portfolio should be made up of stocks. Using this as a guide, along with your time horizon, will help you figure out the best way to allocate your assets.

Key takeaway: Knowing how long you've got to invest, and how well your stomach and sleep patterns can handle risk, will help you figure out how much of your portfolio to invest in stocks.

On the issue of diversification we differ from Buffett's opinion. Whereas Buffett has long believed that you need to own just a few stocks, and own a whole lot of each of them, we believe in spreading things out a bit more. In this way, we tend to be a little more like Peter Lynch or Ben Graham than Buffett.

We're not suggesting you run out and buy shares of 1,000 companies (that's how many Lynch left behind in his Magellan Fund once he'd retired!), or even 100. There'd be no way you could keep up with all those companies. But we do believe that a portfolio of at least 15–20 companies reduces the risk that something horrible will happen with one of them that could sink your entire portfolio.

Buffett believes that by concentrating on just a few stocks, versus buying many, you actually reduce your risk because you are more likely to buy stocks you know a lot about and believe in more fully. We still want you to buy companies you understand and know as much as possible about. We just believe that it's easier to protect your precious capital when you don't have it sitting in so few places. Things go wrong all the time with companies, or the economy, or some specific industry or segment of the market. Having your money spread out among many investments means that if one of them goes bust, the others should (hopefully) be able to offset it.

One easy way to get instant diversification is something Buffett does strongly advocate, though, and that's investing in an index fund. An index fund is a mutual fund that exactly follows an index of stocks. So, for example, an index fund that tracks the S&P 500 will include all 500 of the various companies held in the index. When you buy shares in an index fund, it's like owning a slice of all those companies, and therefore, all those various industries and business types and so forth. You get the benefit of being exposed to many companies in one easy transaction.

Now, the managers of an index fund will not try to "beat the index" or "beat the market." Instead, their aim is to match it. That may sound like a yawn, but consider the fact that according to Motley Fool research only 42 percent of actively managed funds beat the S&P 500 through the fifteen years ending January 2009. Not only that, but index funds are typically very low cost, which means you save money versus investing in an actively managed fund. So you make more and save more when going with an index fund. For something that only seeks to match the market's average return, that's not bad. Average never looked so good, in fact.

We believe you should stick some money in an index fund, in addition to investing in individual stocks. Even if it's just through your company's retirement plan (what? you aren't investing in your 401{k}? what's wrong with you?), an index fund is the perfect foundation for your entire investment strategy. Buffett thinks so, and so do we.

Key takeaway: Diversification, both through owning 15–20 individual stocks and through owning shares of an index fund, is a very good thing. It helps reduce your risk and protect your portfolio.

■ WHAT, ME SELL?

We've just spent many words and many minutes of your time telling you to never sell, basically. And that's still great advice. Buffett's favorite holding period is forever and so is ours.

But the dirty little truth is that sometimes you simply must. It can be painful to say goodbye to a company you've taken the time to get to know, but sometimes you just have to. And here are some situations where that makes sense.

First, you will, from time to time, come across better opportunities. Your goal as an investor is to have each and every dollar maximized and invested in the best possible place. If that means selling a current holding, even for a loss, to make that happen, you just have to do it. Sometimes you need to free up money for a better opportunity, and selling something you currently own to raise the cash to do so is your best option.

Even Buffett has had to part with stocks he likes to be able to invest in new opportunities. He did this in 2009 when he sold shares of Johnson & Johnson and Procter & Gamble to raise money for his huge Burlington Northern acquisition.[6] There's no shame in that. Your resources are finite, after all, so do what you must to deploy them efficiently.

Next, you may need to consider selling thanks to changes at a company you've invested in. Unfortunately, there's just no way around it: Businesses change, and sometimes significantly. We could be talking about a major acquisition, a change in management, a shift in the competitive landscape, or a change in the company's direction or focus. When this happens, incorporate the new information and reevaluate to see if the reasons you bought the company in the first place still hold true. Remember how we talked earlier about writing down the reasons you bought a stock in the first place? That's where this documentation will come in handy for you. Pull out that raggedy old notebook with SpongeBob SquarePants on the cover to help remind yourself why you bought this company, and to see if things have changed dramatically for it.

When you're thinking about the company, consider selling if:

- Its ability to crank out profits is damaged or clearly fading.
- Management undergoes significant changes or makes questionable decisions.
- A new competitive threat emerges or competitors perform better than expected.

You should also take into account unfavorable developments in a company's industry. Here it's important to delineate between temporary and permanent changes. In a downturn, the financial results of even the best-run companies may suffer. What's important is how these businesses take advantage of the effects on their industry to improve their competitive position.

The third reason you may consider selling a stock is for valuation reasons. Now, granted, we're all for long-term buy-to-hold, but sometimes Mr. Market just shows our stock too much love. (Our stock is shy and doesn't like all that attention!) When that happens, consider selling if the stock price has run up to a point where it no longer reflects the underlying value of the business.

Our fourth reason starts with a whoops. Hey, everyone makes mistakes, as we've seen—even Buffett. Sometimes, you'll just plain miss something. You'll get something wrong, you'll be too excited about the heady prospects for the "next big thing," or you'll just generally slip up in some other way. It happens. When it does, you should seriously consider selling if it turns out your rationale for buying the stock was flawed, if your valuation was too optimistic, or if you underestimated the risks.

The final reason to think about selling a stock is what it's doing to your ability to sleep well at night. We talked earlier about how much risk you're comfortable taking on, and sometimes you can overestimate that. It's tough to put a dollar value on your peace of mind. If you have an investment whose fate has flipped this way and flopped that way such that it now causes you to lose sleep, that could be a great cue to move your dollars elsewhere. We save and invest to improve our quality of life, after all, not to develop ulcers. Adding insult to injury, stressing about a stock might cause you to lose focus and make rash decisions elsewhere in your portfolio. Remember, there's no trophy or prize for taking on risk in investing. Stick with what you're comfy with.[7]

Key takeaway: Sometimes, you just have to sell a stock you've bought. That's OK, so long as you're doing it for the right reasons.

■ A WORLD OF MEN AND WOMEN, INVESTING TOGETHER.

Finally, a word of advice for all of us investors, men and women alike. Let's take this chance to learn from one another.

For women, you can learn from men to take action, rather than waiting to start investing. We've all heard the statistics, right? Women outlive men by 5–10 years and earn less than men do during their working life, so they need to be saving more for their retirement. Not only are women starting out further behind, but we've got to make do with less. And our risk-averse nature can mean we often don't invest as aggressively as we need to. So it is critical that more women take control of their financial futures and start investing on their own. Men are more willing to jump in than we are, and we need to remedy that. We've just seen that women are wired for investing success, so take advantage of that fact!

Now, of course, we're not saying you should start investing and begin trading like a madwoman. But you've got to make the moves necessary to get in the investing game. Finding and opening a discount brokerage account isn't difficult. There are many that offer low minimum balances and cheap trades. You can check out Fool.com's Broker Center for comparison tables and links to them. Once you find one you like, it takes only minutes online to fill out the forms. Honestly. You've no excuse not to do it.

After you open your account, start by buying one share of a stock. Yes, just one. Make it something you're interested in, a company you know well and can have fun following. Think about consumer brands or retail companies, to start. Handbag company Coach, for instance, has been a stellar performer, even through the recent recessionary times. Or warehouse store giant Costco, which we discussed earlier, is an outstanding company. There are tons of examples all around you. Find one you like—and *do it*. Take action.

Once you make your move, keep reading everything you can about the company. Track its quarterly results and business performance. Notice how amazing it feels to own a share of a business. It can, and should, be fun!

Now, don't stop with one. Keep on going. Build your portfolio. Follow your holdings. Remember to keep the proper temperament. And smile. You are an investor. You've taken hold of your financial future, and you should be proud of that.

Now, men can learn something from women, too. As

we've talked about through this entire book, the most important factor in long-term investing success is having the right temperament. And men, while they are likely to take action, are then likely to take too much of it, and sabotage their very chances. Men, trade less. Take less risk. Tone down your overconfidence. It's affecting your decision making and could possibly even be causing trouble for the financial world at large. You may not be able to rid yourself of testosterone, but try to overcome its win-at-any-cost effects. The market swings and binges of the past will hopefully become less likely in the future, if only men could learn a little something from the fairer sex.

Ladies, you're not off the hook, though. You can't just sit back and rest on your good temperament's laurels. You've got to start investing, and putting your excellent temperaments to work for you. After all, while Warren Buffett may not, in fact, be a woman, he does invest like one, as we've now seen. You've got the natural inclination to follow in his footsteps. And you can build the skills to do so. Don't waste this opportunity. One day, perhaps we'll be reading a book about your investing prowess and your name will sit alongside the Oracle's. It's possible, but not until you start investing. Make that day today.

Appendices

A Quick Guide Recapping the Female Investor's
  Temperament and What Buffett Can Teach Us

Interview with Value Investor Lisa O'Dell Rapuano, CFA,
  Founder of Lane Five Capital Management

Interview with Value Investor Lauren C. Templeton, Founder
  of Lauren Templeton Capital Management

Interview with Value Investors Candace King Weir and
  Amelia Weir of Paradigm Capital Management

Interview with Value Investor Bill Mann of the Motley Fool
  Independence Fund and the Motley Fool Great America
  Fund

Further Reading: Books for Investors of All Levels Who
  Want to Learn More (Courtesy of *Motley Fool Inside Value*)

A QUICK GUIDE RECAPPING THE FEMALE INVESTOR'S TEMPERAMENT AND WHAT BUFFETT CAN TEACH US

Female investors tend to:

1. Trade less than men do
   - Remember you're buying a piece of an actual business.
   - Take the long view.
   - Be patient.

2. Exhibit less overconfidence: men think they know more than they do, while women are more likely to know what they don't know
   - Buffett's "sphere of understanding" may be different from your own.
   - Think about and learn what your own circle of competence covers.
   - Stick to it, no matter what.

3. Shun risk more than male investors do
   - Insist on an appropriate margin of safety.
   - Avoid debt as much as possible.
   - Stay within your circle of competence.
   - Do your homework before investing overseas.

4. Be less optimistic, and therefore more realistic, than their male counterparts
   - Be levelheaded about your investments and the market at large. Learn not to be excited by market swings to the upside or devastated by market drops.
   - You're in charge of Mr. Market. Don't let him boss you around.
   - Quoting Buffett, "When investing, pessimism is your friend, euphoria the enemy."

5. Put in more time and effort researching possible investments, considering every angle and detail, as well as considering alternate points of view
   - Read, read, read.
   - Don't forget about your circle of competence.
   - Avoid confirmation bias—seek out information that contradicts your conclusions, not just information that reinforces them.

6. Be more immune to peer pressure and tend to make decisions the same way regardless of who's watching
   - Be willing to be contrarian, as uncomfortable as it may be.
   - Take Buffett's words to heart: "Be greedy when others are fearful, and fearful when others are greedy."
   - Live by your own Inner Scorecard.

7. Learn from their mistakes
   - You're going to make mistakes. We all do. So don't beat yourself up when you slip up.
   - Assess what happened. Did you miss something? Or did market conditions change?

- Think about what you can reasonably do differently in the future. If you bought stock in a company you didn't truly understand, for example, vow not to do that again.

8. Have less testosterone than men do, making them less willing to take extreme risks, which in turn could lead to less extreme market cycles.

While not a trait of the female investing temperament, the outcome of this investing style is important. Therefore, remember that female investors produce results that are more consistent and persistent. And in the hedge fund world, female-managed hedge funds outperform comparable male-managed hedge funds, and they don't suffer from market drops as severely.

- Ignore anyone who tells you throwing darts at a newspaper is the same as intelligent analysis.
- A good defense is just as valuable as a good offense.
- Stick to a system that's logical and works, and you, too, could build a lengthy and impressive track record.

And our three Buffett-centric principles:

1. Value and cultivate your relationships with people
   - A business is only as strong as the people running it.
   - Read up on the management of companies you are considering investing in. Look for smart, open, loyal, fair executives you can admire.
   - Don't be afraid to put people before profit; Buffett isn't.

2. Learn from the masters, but be willing to question them
   - The learning never stops, so even after you think you've figured out the best way to invest, keep studying.

- Just because someone's an acknowledged investment guru or master doesn't mean there isn't a better way.
- You aren't committing blasphemy when you question anybody, Warren Buffett included.

3. Be fair and operate in an ethical manner
   - You can be good and be rich; one doesn't preclude the other.
   - It's possible to find companies where employees, shareholders, and customers all win, and those can make for winning investments.
   - Look for companies that communicate in an open, honest way. You, as an owner, deserve to be treated this way.

INTERVIEW WITH VALUE INVESTOR LISA O'DELL RAPUANO, CFA, FOUNDER OF LANE FIVE CAPITAL MANAGEMENT

Lisa Rapuano founded Lane Five Capital Management in January 2007, after years spent at the legendary value shop Legg Mason Capital Management. Based out of Towson, Maryland, her firm's seven core values evoke a true Buffett-like temperament and outlook. We discuss some of those values, and much more, in the interview that follows, which I conducted with Lisa on September 10, 2010. It has been published as transcribed.

Tell me a little bit about Lane Five Capital Management and what you and your team are working to achieve there.

Lane Five is an investment partnership. We're structured as a hedge fund but we don't really hedge much. We have the capability to short and we don't really short much. What I've tried to do is create a firm that has the freedom to do true long-term value investing. While that sounds silly, because isn't that what we're all trying to do, I've been through a number of iterations and it's hard to create the institutional freedom to do it the right way. And the pressure to manage to an index or to not hold cash or to trade around events or to manage month-to-month returns or to not have tracking error is endless. It's really hard to build a business without playing that game. I'm attempting, then, to create a firm that can carve out a little bit of freedom away from some of these institutional constraints so that we can practice our craft. That's why the structure of our firm is the way that it is.

There are a couple of other items, such as, I personally decided at some point in my life that I didn't want to manage $25 billion when I grew up and that the process of asset gathering and also of just meeting the needs of that much money and investing directly with that much money was more than I could handle. So, Lane Five is a small firm. We have the capacity to be many times the size that we are, but even if we were many times the size that we are, we would still be a small firm. So this idea of being a small partnership is sort of designed so that we can be successful while still staying small and investing the right way to invest.

How did you end up as a value investor? Did you explore other investment styles before "seeing the light"?

I didn't really think about the definition of what I am until my career was well under way. The guy who first hired me, he didn't even hire me to be a research analyst. It was this little firm called Franklin Street Partners in Chapel Hill [North Carolina] and the guy was Bob Eubanks. I was the third employee. His firm was a start-up and he hired me to write the brochure. I also built the computer system—it was a start-up, so I did whatever needed to be done. He had an interesting style. There was a value component to it but it was much more story driven, he used a lot of charts, he cared a lot about growth. He was looking for stocks that go up, basically. That was my first exposure to investing. Over time, I started doing research for him.

When I left there and started working for Bill Miller [at Legg Mason], that was 1993. So, in 1993, Bill was not famous, not well-known yet. I came in there and I learned from Bill a more valuation-centric and driven part of the same way of looking at things. Let's differentiate valuation from value— valuation was a central part of the strategy at Franklin Street that I learned from Bob. It wasn't so much, "Is it a value stock?" It was more, "Where's it trading, what is the valuation, and where should it be?" which is, in fact, value investing but it doesn't necessarily go about it the way that, "Let's look at what Graham and Dodd did. Let's look at what Buffett does. Let's structure this philosophically from the bottom up." It approached it a little bit differently.

Then you fast-forward to the Bill years, which is really where I became a more mature investor. We were totally grounded in valuation, but I didn't even read Ben Graham until 1997. So what's interesting about it is that I don't have that background of so many other value investors.

One of the guys I just hired just came from Columbia and Buffett and Graham are everything. Everything. The basis of the universe. I come to some of the same conclusions and practices but without the moral grounding, I guess is the way I would say it. For me, it's not "This is the way that Buffett does it. This is the way that Graham did it. This is the way that I'm going to do it, damn it!"

Valuation was really, really important and was *the* driving factor of what we did at Legg Mason but our outcomes and what we ended up doing were very different than what other people who called themselves value investors were doing. Just like I don't spend a lot of time thinking about what animal we're in—bull, bear, duck, whatever—I don't spend a lot of time thinking about "I'm a value investor." The valuation is all that matters and I learned that from coming in from a different direction. It doesn't matter what it does, who it is, who runs it. All that matters is, is it mispriced? And the only way to figure out if it's mispriced is to use valuation. So, I came at it a little backwards.

The most appropriate Buffett quote that I learned afterwards is that all investing is value investing, because, by definition, nothing is going to go up more than the market if it's not mispriced at the initial position.

Warren Buffett's been quoted as saying temperament— not intellect—is the most important quality an investor can have. How do you think your own temperament has played into your success as an investor?

I think there's a couple things. Let me start by talking about the portfolio attributes I've chosen. You choose to manage money the way that you think you can make a difference, that fits your temperament and your style. I am very good at ignoring noise, the day-to-day stuff just isn't important, and I will go months without trading. I'm not sure how people who trade every day and are looking at short-term trends and optimizing trading strategies and things like that sleep at night. For me, it's patience, it's low activity, it's thoughtful, it's moving more deliberately. I don't know why I have been particularly good at doing that, but I do know that it's an advantage that I have over a lot of people. I just don't feel the need to "do something" a lot of times.

Now, I don't know if that's a learned behavior or an inherent behavior. I think it's probably a little bit of both, because I'm not the mellowest person in the world who just sits around and, you know, listens to the Grateful Dead. I'm actually extraordinarily competitive and I'm also a sprinter—not even a long-distance runner, which would seem to make more sense. But that requires a great deal of patience and discipline and work, even though your race is only twenty-three or sometimes twenty-four seconds long. So I think that it's simply that to me, that is the best way to manage your own emotions, that is the best way to lower your number of mistakes, and it simply makes sense to me. So I can't say that the low-activity, long-term-thinking thing is a personality trait but I definitely adopted it because I think it's the one that works.

Another thing, and I think this is probably more temperament than learned behavior, I care a lot about figuring out something and very little about what other people think and so I've always been a little bit unconventional. So that piece of my personality and that piece of my temperament is suited to the long-term value investing way. Once I figure something out and I put something together and I have a lot of confidence I can ignore what everyone else has to say—I don't ignore evidence—but I can ignore the noise and the opinions of people and continue to build my confidence. That's not hard for me. That's something I find to be very easy. That could come from training as a history major, looking for long-term trends and threads of truth.

Buffett talks about judging himself strictly by an inner scorecard, not an outer, meaning he doesn't care what anyone else thinks. Isn't it hard at times to operate that way, though?

When you're not doing well, in the shorter term, which can happen to anyone, sometimes it's because you're making mistakes, sometimes it's because you're not applying your process correctly, but sometimes you are and you still aren't doing well. You have to combine these two things of being adaptive, open-minded, and being a learning machine with also not changing your stripes or chasing the latest trend. It's a really fine line, a really difficult line to walk.

There's a lot of successful investors of all stripes but my particular strength and my particular adoption of long-term value is because there are kinds of things where I can see a different future than other people see. I can have confidence in something where the market is discounting complete uncertainty. There's an evidence-based part of it and an analytical-based part of it but there's also a time horizon part of it where I want to look through and see how this is going to shake out. I'm going to look at how lots of other things have happened in the past and use my ability to look far and wide to do that and I think that part comes from having this drive to understand things, whether that's from reading history or understanding why science works—I don't care, whatever tool I have to use to figure it out, I will use it. Having this sort of multidisciplinary viewpoint about the world helps with that.

Which investors have you admired and learned from? What lessons have they taught you?

I admire and learn from anyone who has a really good record and I try to figure out how they got there. I'll read an interview with anyone and ask myself what do I have in common with this person and what do I not, and why *not* do it that way? I use these as opportunities to figure out how I could do something better but there are obviously some people I bond with more than others. It's interesting; they're not necessarily the ones who do it just like I do.

Obviously, Bill Miller is my hero. He gave me the building blocks to build my career, and he and I work together very, very well. And we created a process when I was at Legg Mason from 1993 to 2003 that I think was exceptional. I learned from him and he learned from me, I hope, a little bit. We had a very wonderful time.

Bill is the only one of these people I actually know. All these others I don't know. I read what they do and I look and say, "Parts of what they do has helped me do what I do better." The weirdest one of these is Bruce Berkowitz. When he talks, it's like it's coming out of my mouth and yet we never own the same stocks, either. It's just when he talks philosophically I really feel a camaraderie with him.

I have learned a lot from reading the ones that everybody reads, the Seth Klarmans and the Ben Grahams and the Warren Buffetts. And I try to take what they're saying and learn from them, but what's different about me is that I don't try to be these guys. I don't take everything they say as gospel. Because it's what suits them and that's why they're good. They found what they're good at.

I don't think you can adopt someone else's style. I don't have an investing idol, someone I'm trying to be just like. I try to learn from each of them, and I think how am I different from this person and how am I different from this next person?

Even if you talk to Bill Miller, who I'm still very close with, he will tell you all the things that are wrong with me, one of which is that I have too high of an evidentiary threshold, meaning I have to do a lot more analytical groundwork before I'm comfortable with something. I need a higher degree of certainty than he does. But if you look at my degree of certainty that I need, it's probably much, much lower than what Buffett needs. Or what Seth Klarman needs.

So I read them all and I think they're all amazing. Some of my favorite people to read are also the ones who are out of favor. I try to find out, "How do they react in times of adversity?" All of these guys who have records that are really good, and better than mine right now, probably—they all have something to teach me. I try to figure out which of the things that they're doing are applicable to my skill set, my temperament, my firm, and my team. And if it works, I will try to adapt to incorporate it.

I think this is an important point, because as we talk about in the book, Buffett started out as pure Ben Graham, but he would become more qualitative and more Phil Fisher–like over the years, thanks largely to Charlie Munger's influence. It's important for people to realize that they can and should learn from the established masters, but they should never be afraid to do things their own way.

Right. You come from a different set of experiences, you come from a different generation, you have a different education, you have a different brain, you have different parents. So what drives me crazy is pure Buffett worship. Sure, Buffett's great, he has a great record, but he's not going to tell you everything that's going on in his head. You can't replicate it, you can't copycat. This business is way too competitive to try to be what somebody else is being. As I said at the Value Investing Congress one year, "I am not Warren Buffett and neither are you." So just be careful not to try to be someone else. Figure out your own place and just be yourself.

In the list of core values for your firm, Lane Five Capital Management, you list "Work with brilliant people." We know Buffett also values his relationships, whether he's buying an entire company and leaving the current management intact, or buying a piece of a public company with a management team he admires. Two questions about this, then—how do you define "brilliant" and how do you suggest the average investor try to assess the management of companies he or she's investing in?

There are three kinds of different people you work with in our business. There's your team, the people who work for you or work with you. There are your clients. And then there are the companies you're invested in and the people there. We try to apply that core value to all three.

I define "brilliant people" in the following way: For the people who work for me or with me, the other partners in the firm—their brilliance doesn't have to be the same as my brilliance. There is a pure intellectual firepower issue there. The most important piece is curiosity and having a broad range of interests, and having a fire in the belly to figure stuff out, whether it's cognitive psychology, or the best mechanism for where you put your hand when you bring the free throw up, or economics or political science or whatever. A thriving curiosity is the single most important piece for me, because even if the person has a few points' lower IQ, if they've got that thriving curiosity, they'll make up for it. I like voracious readers. I like people who have done lots of interesting things.

Back to the unconventional thing, I really don't like people who have had a career that is just what they tell you to do—Ivy League, Goldman Sachs for two years, business school, try to get a job at a hedge fund. Those people don't interest me. So that's how I define brilliance. And the reason this is one of our core values is that I have a style that's not for everyone, as a client, either. So what happens is that there's a self-selection mechanism for the people who are my limited partners—my partners in my fund versus my partners in my firm. They tend to be people who I enjoy talking to, also. I can't tell you how amazing that is to have happen.

And then there's the management piece. I bend the rules a little bit here because brilliance has lots of different ways of manifesting itself. In fact, I've found that just because somebody's a really smart guy or girl, that doesn't mean they're a great manager of a company. So what I'm assessing on that side is almost always just whether they are very good at capital allocation. That's not just whether or not you buy back stock or what kind of debt you use. That's also what R&D you fund, how you choose to grow, do you understand earning excess returns in your business, and do you understand when it's appropriate not to invest. So I judge the quality of management almost exclusively on whether they get that capital allocation piece of the pie.

I try to judge that first without meeting them, because

a smooth person can really mess you up a little bit. If I'm investing in a company that's not necessarily a turnaround, that's more just an ongoing business, where I can look at the record and make a reasonable assessment of it, I try to judge it mathematically. What have they done? Have they bought back stock when it made sense? Have they levered up when it made sense? Have their acquisitions been value-added? Have they improved returns on capital? Are they good at that? That's a significant measure as to whether that's good management or not.

Then there's the ones where you have to ask, "Are they *going* to get it?" That's a much more difficult assessment to make. Then you're relying on human judgment, which is the least reliable of the tools that we have. I also have a lot of stupid rules about certain types of managers I just don't want anything to do with. They're things like, "What is their behavior like? Are they really promotional? Do they seem to be too geared up on growth? Are they too slick around the edges? Are they too salesy on the whole thing?" You know, basic questions about integrity. I prefer sort of boring people who are low-key, down-to-earth, and interested in doing the right thing rather than convincing me that they're the greatest thing since sliced bread.

For an average investor, they can do the mathematical thing that I do, which is look at their history of capital allocation. That's something that anyone can do, because you just need the 10-Ks to do that. But the objective judgment of a management team is much tougher. You can't really tell from seeing a guy on CNBC if you can trust him or not.

You can learn a lot from the conference calls, though. You can learn a lot from how they answer the questions, whether they answer them straightforwardly, and how they frame their answers, whether they're aggressive or conciliatory. But you are a little bit out of luck, as an individual, not having access necessarily to them. And frankly, even as a small firm, I don't always have access to CEOs and CFOs. I usually have to win my way into their hearts by proving that I've done all the work and that often takes a long period of time. Eventually I get in. Sometimes it takes a lot of phone calls, though, asking questions that the IR person can't answer to demonstrate my interest and my integrity and the work that we've done before finally getting the CEO or the CFO to pay attention.

Every once in a while, you come across a management team that just gets it. For example, when Ed Breen took over Tyco in 2002 the company at that time was a disaster. He would just get on the call, and this is a very complicated company, and he would talk about it in terms that were simple but not simplistic. He narrowed it down to the key elements. You'd get off his conference calls and think, "You know, it's just not that hard. Why do other companies have to make it so hard?" You'd wonder, "How come this guy gets it?" and then you'd listen to another call, where maybe they listen to Wall Street too much, maybe they don't understand their constituents, they think they have to change their story. You'd just come off and think, "He doesn't get it. He doesn't get how to drive this particular business and how to communicate it to Wall Street in a simple manner. Or he's just trying to tell us what we want to hear."

I think anybody can listen to conference calls and determine, "Does this person sound like they really understand their business and if I worked for him would I do what he says? Would I be excited and on board?" There's just a yes or no. Does the management get it or does the management not get it? Believe it or not, there are more companies where the management doesn't get it than there are where they do.

Another of your firm's core values is "Learn and read widely." This is also something that Buffett's legendary for, as is his partner Charlie Munger. Why do you think this is important?

It matters because the world is complex and the world is adaptive. I don't know why this is, I don't have a theological or epistemological foundation for this, but it has come to my attention time and time again that there are patterns in the world that repeat across seemingly unrelated systems. So there are things about the markets that appear to me to be very similar to the way that biological systems work. Or there are analogies, there are recurring patterns that are similar, and we sure know a lot more about biological systems than we do about the markets, and so if I can study biological systems and they can give me any little insight into how this works, that's helpful. And it's really indirect, so I don't want to make it sound like, "Well, I study nerve systems and I figure out that this works that way." It's really very indirect and very amorphous.

There's also the element of historical patterns, not just systems, but events, such as the way that wars happen, the way that cultures evolve, the way that demographics have affected countries, the way that natural events have affected countries—again, amorphous, indirect, but they provide greater connections in your brain, your brain becomes more robust, and the pattern recognition machine becomes better.

You make connections that other people might not make. That's at a very broad level.

At a more practical level, a curious person is more likely to uncover the piece of information that will be the evidence you need to have higher confidence than the next guy that is not curious enough to be resourceful. You know, someone who's basically like, "I get this. I understand how this works. I don't need to think about it all that much." Whereas someone like me, or the people who work for me, are always asking, "How else can I think of that? What am I missing? What else is happening? What else could I do? How else could I turn this on its head? What else could I research to figure out if this is right or not?"

Now, you have to be careful with that, because you could work on one thing 12 hours a day for the rest of your life and still not have 100 percent information. But it's the drive to be curious, and the person who naturally wants to learn and read widely is more likely to be a better analyst. Then, secondly, the act of reading widely and broadly provides you with a more robust set of patterns and connections and networks that, at the margin, I think help you understand how the world works.

What do you read every day?

Well, every day is less important than over time, but every day you do have to do your defensive reading. You have to keep up with what's going on, and read the business news, which is annoying, but you have to. That is more defensive than offensive.

There's a couple of big categories of things, so let's look at my kind of reading schedule. Number one, I always keep room for reading novels and I know that might sound like a girly

thing to say. I'll let the boys all read history and biographies—
I know that because I just interviewed five hundred people,
and every boy, when you ask them what they like to read, they
all say, "biographies." I keep room for novels, though, because
I think novels are insights into human psychology and I enjoy
them and they help you get off your 10-Ks and 10-Qs. I'm
very wary of people who say I don't have time to read novels
because I have so many 10-Ks to read.

Outside of that, there are three categories. First is science.
I belong to the Santa Fe Institute, which is something that Bill
[Miller] introduced me to. It's for the study of complex adaptive systems and I really, really love it. I don't understand 80
percent of it, but I love it. And it's, again, sort of indirect and
amorphous—you let it wash over you and occasionally something comes out where you go, "Oh my gosh, I understand
now how this works." So I enjoy reading about science. It'll
vary—I'll go through an evolution period, I'll go through a
psychology period, I went through a big brain period last year.
Climate stuff is really fascinating to me, too.

Another category is strategic or competitive—these are
more business books, but they might not be 100 percent about
business. They might be about different competitive ways of
looking at the world. It might be rereading [Michael] Porter's
Competitive Strategy. It might be reading any books about how
industries develop and how to think about competitive posi-
tioning. That's also reading Michael Eisner's book, or reading
Disney War, or reading *Good to Great*, or Roger Lowenstein's
books—those sorts of books, where you don't always have to
read the whole thing, but they can give you insight into how
a business works and they're really helpful. Then, I'll do a lot
of behavioral finance stuff—that might not be books as much

as papers, going back and reviewing some of the stuff that Andrew Lo is doing or those kinds of things.

What are some of your favorite books on investing or business?

Let me tell you the books that I reread. The ones that I read over and over again are Peter Bernstein's *Capital Ideas*, the first six or seven chapters of Robert Rubin's uncertainty book (you can stop once you get to the part about Latin America—I'm talking about where he lays out probabilistic thinking in the beginning), the Jesse Livermore book, *Education of a Speculator, Moneyball*. I've read a million other books, but I don't go back and reread *Security Analysis*. I actually would go back and read *The Intelligent Investor* more than I would *Security Analysis*. Those are the ones I reread. The ones I remind myself, maybe not every year, but maybe every other year or so, just to remind yourself why you do what you do.

What's been your biggest mistake as an investor? What did you learn from it?

I have made so many mistakes I have a hard time picking one. But I can tell you that they are, essentially, all the same mistake. First, there are two things you need to differentiate in our business: There's being wrong, and there's making mistakes. They are not the same thing. I really focus on process versus outcome.

Being wrong is when you applied the process correctly, and the outcome was bad. You look back and you say, "OK, well, based on the information I had at the time, would I have made the same decision?" If you determine that you applied your process correctly and that you did the best you could and you just made the wrong decision with the right process, fine. Accept it and move on.

The ones that are bad outcomes because of bad process—or sometimes you can even have good outcomes with bad process, but we'll focus on the bad outcomes and bad process—those are the ones you have to really worry about.

Here's a recent example of that. I've made others, but I'll give you a recent one. I lost a lot of money in 2008 in a lot of things, but the one that drives me bananas was investing in the Renault stub—you know, the car. Our analysis was actually good. It's not like there was anything about Renault that we didn't know or understand, that we didn't get. This was a trade where you buy Renault and then you short Volvo and Nissan against it because they owned 44 percent of Nissan and 20 percent of Volvo Truck, so you could basically create Renault's core business for free. So then 2008 happened, the economy tanked and obviously car companies would do particularly badly at that particular moment so we ended up losing a lot of money because not only did it go down, but Renault went down more than Nissan and Volvo. So a stub that was trading for zero went into massive negative trading. So fine, it's an understandable mistake—how could you have known the economy was going to fall apart? I'm not beating myself up over that part.

The two things I did in that mistake that absolutely drive me to distraction are, No. 1, I normally save myself from massive errors like bankruptcy and things like that by avoiding businesses like car businesses. I will do turnarounds, I will do messy things, but I don't usually do *that*. As I look back on it,

I think probably because things that appeared cheap to me at that point were few and far between, at the beginning of '08, I overdid it on this one. I put way too much of my portfolio in it because it was so cheap and it was so easily explainable. So it was putting too much in it, in a business that wasn't a good business, so when you are wrong you don't get saved by the goodness of the business.

And here's the additional lesson—probably the one that's going to be the easiest never to repeat again—I got so much positive feedback on this one. Everyone said it was brilliant. I presented it at the Value Investing Congress and the whole world was like, "Oh my God, that's the best idea." I'd talk about it in client meetings and they'd be like, "Oh it's so great. It's so wonderful. You're going to make a lot of money on this." It was too easy by half.

Letting your confidence be affected by other people's reaction to it should have been a giant red flag because normally when I invest in something, especially at the beginning, not after it starts working, everyone thinks I'm wrong. No one ever tells me how great it is.

There's a lot of little lessons in there, but the big one I think is that external reinforcement of the idea doesn't make it better. And therefore I probably didn't recognize the imperfections of it. I got overconfident. And we just did terribly. It was awful. Even if it hadn't been going into 2008—so let's take that piece out of it, which is a whole 'nother can of worms—[there was] the overconfidence in a bad business and too large a position. Part of our process is avoiding the things where if you're wrong, the business doesn't help you, and actually hurts you. The nature of the business itself hurts you. It was just stupid.

You mentioned looking around and not finding any ready bargains at the time you did this. Do you feel like you lowered your standards?

Yes, totally. The lesson is "When there's nothing else to invest in, don't invest in anything."

What lessons, if any, did you learn from the market meltdown in the fall of 2008? Have you changed anything about your investing style or approach since then?

Yes and no. We had a terrible 2008. We got caught like everyone else. We started going long way too early. I started getting more aggressive right before Lehman went down. There's a good lesson there about patience. Valuations aren't necessarily fleeting. You don't always have to be buying aggressively into dips. You can be a little bit more patient. That's probably a lesson that all value investors have to learn over and over again. That's sort of a self-reinforcing thing.

But from a "changing" perspective, I'm always a little early. When something reaches a price that I think is a good price I will start buying it and the market might decide to offer it at an even better price for a relatively long period of time before it starts to bottom out. So I just have to accept that that's part of our process, and I can't help it. That's just part of investing. There are times I've looked at and said, "Well, I shouldn't have been so early. I shouldn't have gotten in so fast." But at the same time, that's also part of where our successes have come from, so I can't just eliminate that without eliminating some of our major successes over time. Where I can do better is on what I'm already holding when things start to fall apart. One of the dangers that long-term value investors like me have is that we will look through divots, and differentiating between divots and giant black holes is probably something that I could be better at.

We knew how bad the businesses would get. We didn't react to it at all. There are some businesses, again, that are terrific and you don't want to react but there are other businesses that are not as good and you probably ought to react. We've been much more conscious of describing our businesses when we're buying them up front as to whether these are things you're going to hold through thick and thin or are they things where, should you start to see evidence of deterioration, you need to be a little more aggressive about selling. Or also when they get closer to fair value, be more aggressive about selling.

But we went back and we looked at everything we did wrong and a lot more of it was execution than process. So we didn't change our process much. We added some safety measures. We tried to add some better analysis of downside, but when you have trading downside, or mark-to-market downside, it's different than when you have business downside. So when we looked at it, we said, "Some of the things that caused us to lose money in 2008 will happen to us again, and oh well." And there were some other things that we think we'll be able to be more cognizant of, like deterioration in the businesses that are really not the kinds of businesses that you want to hold through any sort of downturn.

I know 2008 was bad and I don't want to sound cavalier about it, but I'm actually pretty happy that we didn't change too much. I've seen a lot of people that changed everything they did and were reactive and that's really bad. So yes, we learned some things and yes, we changed some applications of our process and we tried to emphasize the things that might have helped us do better, but philosophically the core is still the same. We didn't suddenly decide we're going to be fully hedged. We didn't suddenly decide we're going to be macro traders. We didn't suddenly decide to go short. We said, "We made a very conscious decision to do it this way and that's because that's what we think works for the long term and I still believe that."

If you had one piece of advice to pass along to beginning investors, what would it be?

Don't watch CNBC. That's sort of flip, but the real message is "You have to find your own strategy." You can't copy or react to other people. It's a very self-analytical process. Focus on what you do well and what your skill set is and don't worry about what everybody else is doing.

INTERVIEW WITH VALUE INVESTOR LAUREN C. TEMPLETON, FOUNDER OF LAUREN TEMPLETON CAPITAL MANAGEMENT

As we learned in the third chapter of this book, Lauren Templeton's been investing since she was just a little girl. Given that she is the great-niece of Sir John Templeton, value investing quite literally runs in her blood. Her firm, Lauren Templeton Capital Management, is based out of Chattanooga, Tennessee. I conducted this interview with Lauren on September 22, 2010, and it is published as transcribed.

Tell me a little bit about Lauren Templeton Capital Management. How is the firm structured and what are you trying to achieve?

We're an asset management firm. We were founded in 2001. The firm is 100 percent owned by me, so it's a female-owned firm. We began with one hedge fund product but we've since also moved into the long-only separately managed account business. We are a value investing boutique focused exclusively on global bargain hunting. And, naturally, we're trying to build wealth for our investors and compound their money at the highest rate possible in the market given an acceptable level of risk.

How did you end up as a value investor? Did you explore other investment styles before "seeing the light"?

Well, as you might imagine, because I grew up in the Templeton family we are really a family of value investors. I started buying stocks when I was seven or eight years old. My dad would allow me to buy one share a month of any stock I wanted. He would buy it for me. And then he would take the stock certificate, because at the time they mailed you an actual certificate, and he would mat and frame the stock certificate and hang it on the walls of my room. So when I was a child, my room was literally wallpapered with stock certificates.

At first, like any child would, I bought very familiar companies—like Disney, Wal-Mart, the Gap. I really didn't pay any attention to valuation. But it was very important to have these stock certificates hanging on the walls of my room because all of a sudden, I really did, as a child, think of myself as an owner of one of these companies. I can remember telling friends on the playground that, yes, I did own part of Disney. And they couldn't believe it.

But it was that approach to looking at investing through the eyes of a business owner I think that naturally guides investors into value investing. To me, value investing is a lifestyle. In every other area of my life, I seek to find the best bargain in relation to something's value—whether I'm buying a car or a house, and why wouldn't I do the same in the stock market? I just grew up that way. My family was very thrifty. My dad was very thrifty. He owned a local hardware store and he and my mom saved 50 percent of everything they ever made. Uncle John [Templeton] says he did the same thing. Of course, they were saving for the opportunity to go out and buy shares of businesses that were listed on the stock exchange. If you're buying a part of a business, you want to get the best bang for your buck and go where you find the best value.

So I would say I've always been a value investor. Now, of course, I've read about and studied other investment styles but none of them seemed to resonate with me. I think that value investing is investing in the stock market. Many of the other styles and strategies appear to me to be more speculative. I don't approach the stock market as a casino. I don't gamble in the stock market. I invest in businesses.

Warren Buffett's been quoted as saying temperament—not intellect—is the most important quality an investor can have. How do you think your own temperament has played into your success as an investor?

I completely agree with him, first of all—it is temperament and not intellect. I think some people are born with a natural ability to be better investors than other people. However, I think all investors can improve [their temperaments]. I think what makes a good investor is the ability to control your emotions and some people are just better at that than other people, and there are a host of reasons why. There are so many cool research projects out right now in the field of neuroscience looking at the role of hormones like testosterone and estrogen and neurotransmitters like oxytocin that really affect our decision-making process and might contribute to an investor's ability to control his or her emotions. Some people are just naturally better at that but I also think that everybody can learn to be better at controlling their emotions and at least be cognizant of human behavior.

I think that investors who can control their emotions are going to have better returns. Warren Buffett's great at doing that. And in many ways, he does invest like a woman. He does his research, he's cool, calm, and collected. A lot of men get on a testosterone high and take riskier and riskier bets. I think Warren Buffett is a student of human nature and he can control his emotions much better than the average person.

By studying and reading about human behavior, you can implement some tools to help your investing strategy. For instance, Uncle John always kept a wish list of securities in his desk drawer, and oftentimes, he would have good-til-cancelled limit orders out on these securities at well below market prices. Let's say 30 percent below the market. So when the market would fall in value or there would be a major correction in the stock price and he knew that human nature would make it scary to step in and buy, because the trades were already out there, it's kind of forcing yourself to do what you should do and buy a good company when the stock goes on sale.

I think my temperament has helped me because I'm a very good student of human nature. I'm very cognizant of my biases and I spend a lot of time thinking about how to compensate for them, whether that's having limit orders in on certain securities well below the market or different rules or procedures we have here at the firm to assist me when I know I'm going to be in a stressful situation. I also think that I take more risk than most women do. So I think that has helped me in my investment career.

Your investment firm, and the book you and your husband wrote, are based on the investment style of your great-uncle Sir John Templeton, who was a renowned value investor himself. In what ways is his style of investing distinct from Buffett's?

Both Uncle John and Warren Buffett studied under Benjamin Graham. So they're both going to have that as a common denominator in their investment strategies. But the major difference between Sir John and Warren Buffett is the fact that Sir John pioneered global investing. So he's known as a global investor, and although Warren Buffett has recently made some purchases outside of the United States, he's largely known as a U.S. investor. I think that Uncle John had a competitive advantage over Warren Buffett in that he had a larger universe of stocks to study to find bargain opportunities.

Let me give you an example of why a larger universe of stocks is important. Uncle John was investing in Japan in the early 1960s at P/E ratios of 4x. So he was very early into Japan. U.S. investors started buying into Japan in the 1980s. Of course by that point stocks were overvalued in Japan, there was a huge bubble in Japan, headed toward a big stock market crash. Uncle John was already out of Japan by that time. He'd moved 60 percent of his assets into the United States, around 1981, 1982. At the same time, *BusinessWeek* was proclaiming the "Death of Equities" in the United States.

So because he had a larger inventory of stocks and the ability to invest in any country, he could move from Japan when Japan was getting overheated to the United States when stock valuations were very depressed. And he was capable of avoiding Japan's bubble. I think it just makes more sense to increase your inventory or universe of stocks by looking over-seas.

I think that Warren Buffett's genius is in his investment vehicle. The way he structured Berkshire Hathaway is so smart. Uncle John managed a mutual fund, and managing a mutual fund is very difficult because the tendency of an inves-tor is to withdraw capital at the worst time. So the mutual fund manager has to prepare for capital outflows when stocks are cheap and inflows when stocks are expensive.

We know Buffett considers management very impor-tant and values his relationships with people, whether he's buying an entire company and leaving the current management intact, or buying a piece of a public com-pany with a management team he admires. Two ques-tions, then: Do you share this trait with him? And, if so, how do you suggest the average investor try to assess the management of companies he or she's investing in?

We do share that trait with Warren Buffett. However, we assess a company's management ability based on the numbers. So, studying their financial statements, we're looking for com-panies that are growing faster than their industry, have higher operating margins than their industry, and higher returns on capital. Of course, when we study the company, we're study-ing their compensation structure, we're looking at accounting techniques to see if they're being too aggressive with their ac-counting. A large part of that is simply that we're a smaller firm and we can't afford to go visit every single one of the man-agement teams, but we do speak to them all before we invest.

We get the best information, though, from their competitors. But yes, I think management is extremely important, but we judge that through a study of their financial statements.

You know, even Warren Buffett said, "You should invest in a business even a fool can run because some day a fool will." Also, even though Warren Buffett places a huge degree of importance on management, he also looks at competitive advantage, economic moat, for instance. I think the average investor should look for companies that are growing faster than their industry, have higher operating margins than their industry, and higher returns on capital than their industry. And if they find a company that has those three qualities, they've located a good management team.

Buffett is legendary for the amount of reading he does and information he consumes. What do you read on a regular basis? What are your favorite books on investing?

On a daily basis, I read the *Wall Street Journal*. We always have the *Economist* lying around, all over our house, different editions of it, because it takes a long time to read it so I may still be working on an edition from back in July months later. On the weekends, we get *Barron's*.

When I was a young person, one of the first books I read on investing was [James] O'Shaughnessy's *What Works on Wall Street* and I really like that book. And I read Peter Lynch's books and I enjoyed those. For someone who's more serious about investing, I think *The Intelligent Investor* and *Security Analysis* by Benjamin Graham are must-reads. *Common Stocks and Uncommon Profits* by Philip Fisher is a really good book. Like everyone, we're also reading a ton of data online. We have an online report that comes out on a quarterly basis called the Maximum Pessimism Report that we profile our contrarian investment strategies in and that's been really well received. But I love to read other value managers' newsletters. I like to read the quarterly reports from mutual funds that I own. Really, anytime that I can get my hands on another manager's letters or information that I respect and agree with their strategy, that's very helpful to me.

Buffett's known for staying well within his circle of competence, leaving areas like technology companies largely alone. Do you share this investing trait with him?

Yes, very much so, especially as a value investor. As a value investor, if I can't value it, I can't invest in it. So that kept us out of a lot of financial stocks that were showing up in our screens during the financial crisis. We couldn't get our arms around the balance sheets so we couldn't invest in them. How do you value something if you really don't have a transparent view of the balance sheet? Of course that keeps us out of biotech and industries like that where there's just no good way for us to value the company. So if we can't value it, we can't invest in it.

You're familiar with some of the research about the differences between men and women investors. To you, what's the most interesting aspect of this research?

About two years ago I had the great privilege of participating in a discussion out in California, with about fifteen hedge fund managers. The purpose of the discussion was to discuss freedom and free enterprise, but the discussion was led by neuroeconomist Paul Zak from Claremont University. He's produced some amazing research, which has some financial implications. It just made me so excited about the field of behavioral finance and neuroscience and the differences between men and women and that's really what I've been studying for the past two years. So the books on my bedside table right now are all related to that field. It is really fascinating stuff. I guess I am drawn to it because there are few women in my profession and it is interesting to consider how gender influences my behavior. Also, behavioral finance and value investing are very compatible subjects.

What advice would you pass along to beginning investors?

Start early, start now.

So, start investing at eight years old?

Yes, actually! Compounding is magic. You'll laugh at this, but it's true. My dad told me bedtime stories about the magic of compounding. It is magical, but the magic ingredient is time, so start early. But also, start early because you're going to make mistakes and that's OK, too. But go ahead and make those mistakes.

And then my biggest piece of advice is invest, don't speculate. Approach a purchase of a stock as buying a portion of a business. And if you look at it through the eyes of a business owner you're going to make wiser investments. I wish, for that reason, that every time people bought stock they were still issued a stock certificate. Because something about that, as a child, holding that stock certificate in my hand and having something to put on my wall that represented the share that I owned, it really gave me a sense of ownership in that business. And now with everything electronic and no one has stock certificates anymore, it feels like something investors are more apt to go in and trade because they have less ownership of it. I really like stock certificates.

When I graduated from college, I borrowed a very small amount of money from my father to buy a stock that one of my friends had recommended to me. And I borrowed the money, I bought the stock, and it really crashed in value. I lost a ton of money. I called my dad up and said, "Oh, I'm so sorry, I've lost the money." And he said, "Great! That's exactly what I was hoping would happen! Now you know there are no hot tips in the stock market; this is not a game of gambling. You have to do your homework and make wise investments. This is the best lesson I could have ever taught you. I was hoping that stock would go down in value." It really taught me a lot because I was really upset about it. It's not a casino. If you treat it like a casino then those are going to be your results.

INTERVIEW WITH VALUE INVESTORS CANDACE KING WEIR AND AMELIA WEIR OF PARADIGM CAPITAL MANAGEMENT

Mother-and-daughter value team Candace King Weir and Amelia Weir search for value opportunities through their firm Paradigm Capital Management, which serves high-net-worth and institutional investors. Founded as a small-cap outfit, it has since expanded to offer several different investment vehicles for undervalued companies of all sizes. I conducted this interview with Candace and Amelia on October 7, 2010, and it has been published as transcribed.

Tell me a little bit about Paradigm Capital Management. What's the history of the firm?

CANDACE KING WEIR: It was formed in 1972, so clearly that was a long time ago and I think I formed it when I was too young to know any better. I formed it always with the idea that I enjoy small-cap value investing. That has just always appealed to me where you could understand a company and actually have an evaluation methodology that gave you a comfort level. Didn't mean you always were right, but you had comfort that the process was solid and obviously over thirty-seven years you learn a lot, but I still believe the process is very solid and it is very tangible. I left a smaller firm that had done a lot of very esoteric investing, like in biotech and things that would be the next great fix for something, but would always be selling at 30 times revenues and a zillion times earnings or no earnings. I was never good at that. I guess I am more of a fundamentalist.

Amelia, did you want to add anything to that?

AMELIA WEIR: I grew up, obviously, with a mother who had this in her blood for a long time, in that every time you went to do errands or back-to-school shopping or anything like that, you were inevitably doing a store walk at the same time and checking out inventories or traffic or how long the lines were to check out. So, in that sense, obviously it was something that I was always kind of indoctrinated with. But I actually went to college and was an English major undergrad and didn't really totally ever imagine that I would quite be in this seat at this point.

But I actually started off working as an editor at Paine Webber right after college in equity research and at some point it got a little tiresome to keep correcting analysts' typos. At some point, you would rather be on the actual analytic side than just kind of reading someone else's thoughts. I went to work at Bear Stearns in equity research covering the textile and apparel industries, so companies like Tommy Hilfiger and Polo. I really liked it and decided to go back to business school and really knew at that point that I wanted to be on the buy side. I think you sort of have that iterative process of realizing that at some point you don't want to be reading other people's opinions and at some point, even if you can write the research reports, you would still rather be on the actual decision-making side, and so that led me to where I am today.

How did you end up as value investors? Did either of you try other strategies or other methods before kind of settling into your "value skin," so to speak?

CANDACE KING WEIR: I guess I speak for myself since I have obviously done a lot more years than Amelia. No, I have always had a value tilt. That is one of the reasons I formed my firm. I really didn't understand more esoteric investing. I always kind of believed that EBITDA multiples of free cash flow meant something, and as long as you thought you had a management team that made sense and had a product growth story that you could understand, normally those were the kind of fundamentals that allowed you to be pretty successful over time.

AMELIA WEIR: One thing I am just thinking about, and it is easier to see in hindsight, but when I was covering the textile and apparel industries, it was in the late '90s through 2001, so needless to say, no one cared. Everyone was really fired up about Internet this and Internet that and everything was selling at crazy valuations. The fact that you had these really interesting companies with real businesses and real balance sheets and solid cash flows didn't matter. I just remember the sales guys would be coming around the floor to see which analysts had anything interesting to say. They would walk right by us because they couldn't care less. They wanted the more interesting tech names.

I think even then it gave me a sort of perverse or contrarian appreciation for real companies, obviously seeing how that all played out, but at some point I also think it is hard anytime. It is like going shopping, even from a consumer standpoint. You never want to feel like you are overpaying for something. You like to get something on sale, and I think that there is kind of a similar mindset to that idea of recognizing value and feeling like you got it at the right price and that you actually think it is worth more.

Warren Buffett has been quoted as saying that temperament, not intellect, is the most important quality an investor can have. So how do you think your own temperaments have played into your success as investors?

CANDACE KING WEIR: Hmmm, that is a pretty complex question. I guess I would say I think to be good at this, you have to have a pretty even temperament. I think you have to be able to take a longer view at times. I will just go back to something more fresh in my mind, the debacle at the end of '08 and early '09. I don't think any of us quite knew where things were going to shake out at that point, but you couldn't take yourself out of the game. You had to keep showing up, so to speak, and playing the game.

But I think that is where our mantra, and I think Amelia can speak to this, comes in handy. I say to our analysts, "Head down, steady wins the race." Who knows what this is all going to shake out to, what the final outcome is going to be? But if you stick to what you know you do well, which is speaking with the companies and being able to get to management and say, "Your stock is off 70 percent. Is there any change in your business?" Often they say no. Then you say, "Boy, this is really whacko." But you wouldn't go out and spend every last dime you had because you knew you had to be prudent. I think it takes a certain amount of a steady hand to be successful as an investor.

We never try and market-time. I am not good at it. It wouldn't enter my mind to be a market timer. Sure, I think about the macro issues, but I don't try to time my investments. It is really one investment at a time. That makes sense to me. I guess you have to have a certain set courage of your own convictions, because often you can be wrong for weeks or months. It's not that you really were wrong, but you appear to be wrong. Wall Street is down on, going back to Amelia's story, Wall Street doesn't want to talk about clothing manufacturers. That is really dull. A year later, they may say, "Boy, that is brilliant. We want all we can get." So you do have to have the courage of your convictions, I think to be good. You really have to be grounded.

I think we had a pretty fabulous year in '09, just because we stuck to our knitting when other people were just frozen in the ground. We'd just come in and we'd talk to our companies and if we thought that things were really outrageously out of whack, then we would buy a little more, but fundamentally we are very disciplined. I think discipline is really critical, too. You do have to show up every day, no matter the days you hate it. You say, "I can't bear it." You can't bear to lose any more money. I take it very personally always, but if you don't show up, you don't get to play the game and eventually you are just out of the game.

AMELIA WEIR: 2009 was really amazing if you look at the month-by-month performance, in the sense that we ultimately had a very, very good year performance-wise. I guess I am just reiterating the idea that you have to have a long-term view and you have to have that temperament that is more even keeled and that you listen to yourself and you stick with the original idea that you had, versus being swayed by the market or the news or everyone appearing to run for the exits.

It was in the first quarter of 2009 where I would say, and I would say this more about my mother than myself, I think the cumulative experience helps. But it is temperament as well, of buying more of names that you knew and had a comfort level with versus so many people at that point who were really paralyzed and stayed on the sidelines. So that by the time the market turned, they were then kind of scrambling to catch up in the second half of the year, which at some point you can only make up so much of that with the kind of swing that the markets had. I can't think of a better example of the temperament question in a long time than that period, where you really had to get in there and have your own internal clock that told you it was OK, instead of waiting for everyone else to do it, because that is really where you make the best money.

Management and the "people aspect" of investing are very important to Buffett. When Berkshire buys a whole company, he leaves management intact, or if he is buying shares of a public company, he wants to have management he trusts and believes in. Is that important to you all, too?

CANDACE KING WEIR: Absolutely, yeah.

Why? And then additionally, are there ways for individual investors to try to assess management? How would you suggest they go about that?

CANDACE KING WEIR: Yes, I think it is critical because at the end of the day, if I am any example, we own, maybe at any time, maybe 70 names in our portfolio. So you can't possibly be an expert on every product and every company. That would be a fool's game, so you do have to do a little bit of delegation. You have to think that you have a management team that can understand where they should be in the marketplace and what products are going to drive their business. I am not going to try to get down to that next granular level of tell me why XYZ is the next whatever, so I think this is a practical approach to it. You can't know it all.

I think, maybe again, it is because of experience, but clearly you just quickly pick up on bright people, articulate people, people that can tell you a really cohesive story and a vision. Even to this day when I talk to a new company and I have no vested interest as I start the dialogue, sometimes after I finish a conversation, I will just kind of put the file down and send it back to the analysts and say, "I don't think so. Maybe you are right, but I don't think it is going to work if I don't think the company can articulate what they do."

So I think you have really got to understand not only can they articulate their business from the investment community side, but most importantly, do they know their business? How do I know? I look at the track record. I guess I feel like I am a trial lawyer. I ask these questions day in and day out. I have already spoken to six companies today. It's what, 3:30? It's a typical day for me, and I am just constantly gauging and listening for the answers, so you do this long enough and you do have a sense of what the right answer should be.

We are sitting with a detailed set of questions from the analysts and saying, "Well, you need to go back and talk about have they renewed their line of credit, have they done this, what are they thinking about that?" So you are constantly grilling them and you realize it is a good management team if they have those answers. When somebody asks me about my business, I like to think I can articulate most of the answers back to them. And if all of a sudden you find somebody who is kind of hemming and hawing or being slightly evasive, it is just my set of rules, but we just kind of drop the name, because you really don't have time.

This is a hard enough game when you think you are getting good information from the management, not inside information, just a clear understanding of their business. If people somehow are not willing to share that with you, we just kind of move on. There are enough smart managements out there, enough good businesses. I would not invest in a company that says, "Yeah, you can read it when we release our 10-Q." I would say, "OK, thank you." And that would be it.

But as to [individual] investors having that access, I think that is hard. It is not like you have inside information, but it is just having the access because you run enough money. I am not Warren Buffett, but people know we are serious investors, let me put it that way, and they know we have done it for a lot of years, so people respect that, for lack of a better term.

AMELIA WEIR: One thing I would say though is that going back, there were times where we may be on the phone with a company, and I can think of a few in more recent months, but there was one where whatever guidance they had put out, they sort of had a trajectory for the year that they needed to really stick pretty closely to it to make their numbers for the year. At some point toward the end of the call, and again, we have a list of questions, and most of them are pretty straightforward, but we asked something like, "So, you think you are on track to hit that"—I am making up the numbers right now—"but you think you are on track to hit that $20 million revenue number for the second quarter?" And the CFO, he paused for about one second longer than normal and was like, "Well," and basically his answer was like, "Yeah." He didn't say anything, he didn't give you tons of information, but on a certain level we both, after we hung up, we were like, "That did not sound good." And the point being, they blew the quarter not too long after that. Then the real trick is acting on it in time, not just patting yourself on the back for having gauged the answer right.

To your point about individual investors, if it is a company that I either don't know well or don't feel like I really have my arms around—and this is something that I think does matter for the random person on the street who wants to invest—you can listen to the replay of the conference call or you can read the transcript. I always find it much more useful to listen to the conference call. Because a transcript is a transcript, if you are just looking for some numbers or clarification, but you kind of want to hear what the tone is in management's voice. You want to hear them during the Q&A period. Sometimes some of the analysts are more aggressive or not, but you want to hear what that dialogue is like and are they defensive or are they a little vague or are they really helpful? I think that none of that is an exact science, but I think again, it lends additional information if you are willing to go through that effort to listen to it.

I think that is very useful. And you're right, it's just tough, it just is. If you are a retail investor and you don't have access to people, you are left a little bit to your own devices, just the conference calls or just public information, but that's a challenge.

CANDACE KING WEIR: It is just very time consuming. By the time you talk to six companies, you have spent six or seven hours of the day on the phone, so it is not something that you do lightly. You have to have enough, I guess, of a weighted interest to spend that time.

Buffett is legendary for the amount of reading that he does and the information he consumes, so what do you read on a regular basis, and then what are some of your favorite books on investing?

CANDACE KING WEIR: I read pretty voraciously. I think Amelia can attest to that. There is probably not a weekend in my life I am not up early reading for probably a couple of hours before the day gets going. But normally it is just probably a ton of sell-side notes, notes from my analysts, and my daily reading is strictly all the investment things, whether it is the *Wall Street Journal*, *Investor's Business Daily*, Bloomberg, there are zillions.

But I think the trick is you get so much information overload today that you have got to be able to say this isn't worth my time pretty quickly. You can drown in the information, so I try and limit it, keep it relatively simple.

Sometimes when I sort out my reading at the end of the day before I do it the next morning, I will just sort it in piles. One will be like critical information, earnings, company releases and where someone asks about a company that I own right now that I need to think about. Then the other pile will be for when my brain is a little more relaxed. I can look at this on the weekend, like new investment ideas or more macro thoughts. And there are really two different kinds of the information I need to absorb, so I almost have to do it in a different mindset, if that makes sense.

And that is my typical reading. Critical information right away, which I probably spend a couple hours a day on and then a little more big picture, which I probably spend a few hours a weekend on. And honestly, I don't think I have picked up a book on investing in ten years. That is the truth. I find, personally, I am always in constant overload. It is almost too much information. We probably get research from thirty firms every day. We just filter it out every day. It is a lot of stuff to think about.

Then I think our style is our style, which is really about knowing management, running our own earnings models, making our own kind of hypothesis of why we are doing this investment. So it is not like, let me go read this book and figure out how to do it better, and I am not saying we couldn't do it better. It is not like I think we are so terrific, but there are just so many hours in a day. Now and then I will buy a book and I will say, "Hmmm, when I am on vacation, I am going to take this with me." But I have got to say honestly, I'd rarely ever pick it up.

AMELIA WEIR: Yeah, I unfortunately would have to second that. Once in a while someone will give me a book, and they're like, I thought this was a great book, but it sort of goes back to the fact that you are working so hard while you are working that by the time I am going away, then I really want to read the *New Yorker* or something. I don't want to read a maybe good or maybe bad book on investing.

But one of the things that I think is very useful is—again, there is sort of the usual litany, you are reading the *Wall Street Journal*, you are reading the *New York Times*, you are reading the *Financial Times*—then I think one thing that I do value a lot is sort of a slightly more international perspective. So whether you are reading the *Economist* or the *Financial Times,* in addition to the *Journal* and Bloomberg, because I think again, you just see a slightly more, in some ways, objective take on things. In a way, it is the same pieces of the puzzle, but they are maybe presented in a slightly different alignment, which makes you sometimes think about things differently.

CANDACE KING WEIR: I think that is absolutely true.

AMELIA WEIR: As an example, the *New York Times*, some time in early September, had an article about 3-D printing and how it is being used now for things like prosthetics, that historically have been prohibitively expensive and hard to manufacture and time consuming. And some of the newer printing processes are much faster, much cheaper, and make these things much more accessible.

And because I am obviously always behind on my reading, I was just throwing away some old *Economist*s recently, and I was flipping through one. It was a February issue from this year, and they had a three times as long article on the exact same topic, and that was in February, versus the *New York Times* writing this article in September. That is the stuff that is interesting, where some information is out there and some people decide to focus on it at different times. I think by having that spectrum of reading, that is how something sparks your brain. Obviously, I didn't read that article in February, but I think that stuff is interesting because you never know what kind of alchemy makes something from an investing perspective spark in your own mind, like, "What about this?" Or, "If this is happening here and that is happening there, then what is the implication for palladium mining stocks?" So I think in that way, it is really important to just have that breadth.

CANDACE KING WEIR: And also I would say just that you need to get away, because we are pretty intense when you are working. They are pretty intense days—whether they are ten- or twelve-hour days—they are long days and they are very intense. Sometimes you just absolutely, whether it is being in Timbuktu or being in London or being in Paris, you definitely just need to totally change your environment. And then that does give you a totally fresh look at things.

I think that is critical, too. I know a ton of really bright people who work extraordinarily hard. It doesn't mean it is always successful. That is the irony of life, so sometimes you just have to step back and say, "Whoa, what am I doing here that isn't working?" Because I don't think anyone has the

Holy Grail here. It is just kind of "Do you think you do it better than some people?" Yes, and "Have you done it for a long time?" Yes. "Are you reasonably competent?" Yes, but nobody has the Holy Grail. I think when you can step back, whether it be in Delhi or London, and say, "Whoa, look what they are doing here," you can see all the infrastructure. It is just mind-boggling. Everywhere you looked there were dams and roads and you realized that meant something in a big-picture way that you weren't seeing in Albany, New York, or New York City.

That is great advice. OK, now we know that Buffett is known for staying within his circle of confidence, leaving areas like technology largely alone. Do you all share this investing trait with him?

CANDACE KING WEIR: Absolutely I do. As I get older, I think I should just invest in what I know. Every time we do a once-off, it's like trying to understand some business like we own the company. I won't bore you with a name right now, but we say, "Boy, those are the names you end up losing money on because you don't really have the right peer group kind of perspective." It's not like you know three other people in the business who understand how the business model should work, let alone be able to check out the management team, because other people know them.

Invariably, I would say two out of three times they turn out to be disappointing investments. It maybe takes us a year to figure that out. Whereas if you are investing in your third contract manufacturing company and there are only seven in the whole industry that are public and you know four or five of the seven, then you have a pretty good perspective. I am not saying you are always right, but you know what you should avoid, let me put it that way. I think that is very helpful in life, it's the losses you need to avoid.

AMELIA WEIR: But I would say, well, he [Buffett] avoids technology. That is an area that we are overweight in, so I think again, everyone has their own very subjective sort of . . .

CANDACE KING WEIR: Sense of strength.

AMELIA WEIR: Yeah, exactly, and what kind of grabs someone intellectually or from my kind of curiosity perspective and so in that sense, I think everyone can have their own core competence. But I totally agree that anytime you kind of have dabbled in a name where you really, again, don't have that peer group or competitive landscape or just your own real understanding of it, you are basically weighting things to the downside over the longer term, just because there are more wildcard factors than you can account for versus a retailer when you own ten other retailers.

CANDACE KING WEIR: I think that is right. So we agree with Mr. Buffett.

What advice would you pass along to beginning investors?

CANDACE KING WEIR: As a beginning investor, I would say start where you have some kind of comfort zone, some touchstone that makes you think this makes sense to you. Maybe it is buying shares in the local bank, if you have always done your banking there, or buying ten shares of Nike because you like Nike's running shoes and you think it is a good company. Go somewhere where you have some real tangible thought about the company and not, "So-and-so said to buy this stock because it is going to go up next month."

I remember as a kid, my first stock investment was buying shares in Mohawk Airlines, which was the local regional airline here back in the day. It was just very tangible to me because we flew it all the time. I would have a hard time telling you if I made any money on it or not. I think I did make a little money, but I think that was the idea. What was I, sixteen years old and probably spent $200, but it was very tangible to me, and I think that is important to go with something that at least if it goes wrong, you have a rationale for why you did it as opposed to somebody told me to do it.

Amelia, did you want to add anything?

AMELIA WEIR: I think it's funny that you were just talking about Mohawk. I am thinking about some of my early investing, and again, it was sort of right out of college. I was clearly more of a Luddite and so not so tuned in to the sort of Internet dot.com boom, but I bought, it is amazing, it is sort of like the two stocks you should have never bought, one of which was Xerox. I bought Xerox, and this is obviously as people are starting to use email more and starting to email files to each other. Then the other one, which you know, it was way before the iPod, but it was a music retailer, which again, over time CD sales have fallen off a cliff and no music retailer has ever found a way to really still keep selling hard copies of anything in an upward trajectory.

With that being said, I would say from my first investing experience, they were things that I thought I sort of understood, they made sense to me. I think probably very few new investors are going to be successful, so at least you can look at it and understand why versus you bought something that had dot-com on the end and you bought it for $50 a share and then it went to zero. I still would just stand by the idea that it is something that (a) you use or you are familiar with, or (b) going back to you talking about Nike, it is sort of somewhere that you go, so you might buy Finish Line over Foot Locker as a footwear retailer because you see both in the mall and you always see more people in the Finish Line store. And it may not actually be right, but at least you have the kind of a touchstone that you can keep referring back to, versus it all being in a vacuum.

Yeah, you are starting to think about it and apply cause and effect, in a sense. There are more people in the store, so maybe you could be wrong, but at least you are thinking about it.

AMELIA WEIR: Then if they miss on the quarter and they say, "We were more promotional than we planned on," then that person thinks the next time around, "What is on sale?" and not just how many people are in the store. I think it is sort of that iterative process.

INTERVIEW WITH VALUE INVESTOR BILL MANN OF THE MOTLEY FOOL INDEPENDENCE FUND AND THE MOTLEY FOOL GREAT AMERICA FUND

Bill Mann is the portfolio manager for the Motley Fool Independence Fund and the Motley Fool Great America Fund. He specializes in identifying companies with underappreciated competitive advantages and assets. Prior to working for Motley Fool Asset Management, he served as coadvisor for The Motley Fool's Hidden Gems *and* Pay Dirt *small-cap investment newsletter services and was the founding advisor for The Motley Fool's* Global Gains *international stock newsletter service. Longtime Fool Chris Hill conducted this interview with Bill on September 22, 2010. It has been published as transcribed.*

Buffett has been quoted as saying, "Temperament, not intellect, is the most important quality an investor can have." How do you think your own temperament has played into your success as an investor?

First of all, I have been doing this for a while but I don't know that I'd go so far as to call myself a successful investor yet. I think anybody who does is full of it; probably a little premature if you aren't Buffett's age and at his level of sustained success yet.

That said, I think having a temperament that allows you to worry about the things that are central to a business as opposed to what the stock market is doing is a pretty crucial thing for me. You see people saying all the time, "The market has dropped X percent," or "Some company has gone up 15 percent," like somebody knows something. In most situations, nobody knows anything. It is people being batted to and fro by the waves of the market.

Businesses don't just gain value or lose value as quickly as the market says that they do. I think that is a pretty important thing because it allows people who do have that mentality to find opportunity.

Do you think of yourself as a value investor?

I do. I think of myself as a scaredy-cat investor. I think when you talk about value investing, there are really two ways to look at it. There's the sort of what you'd call statistical value or the people who say, "Well, I am not buying anything unless it is less than a P/E of 7," or, "I am not buying anything above book value." I don't think that way. I think in terms of just trying to buy something for less than it is worth and trying to sell it for what it is worth, or even better, for more than it is worth.

To me, that is the definition of value. As a good example, and I was lamenting this the other day because the company was taken private, in 2005, I recommended a company for *Motley Fool Hidden Gems* (The Motley Fool's small-cap stock newsletter service) called Fairmont Hotels. It had no earnings.

It was in the middle of a restructure. It was a pretty bad time for the hotel business and the stock had done horribly. So if you believed the stock market, this company was on its way out, but there were two things to me that as a value investor I focused on.

One was the fact that this was a company trading at about $2 billion where you couldn't possibly replace all of its hotels for anywhere close to that little. The properties themselves were just worth so much more than $2 billion, so you had some opportunity right there. You had what I would call a floor.

The other thing was that it had cash and so it was not a company that was going out of business, it was just struggling. I think being a value investor gives you the confidence to buy something like that, not really to worry about what is happening over the next couple of quarters. I guess that gets back to sort of the temperamental issue, but it also sort of defines who you are. You are not looking for momentum. You are not looking for companies that are necessarily showing spectacular earnings growth. In fact, their earnings could quite frankly be kind of lousy, but at the same point in time that they are great investments.

How did you get to that point in your investing philosophy? Were there other investment styles that you experimented with before you "saw the light"?

I did a little bit of everything. I have always been fascinated by math and so the graphing and the charting and putting things through sort of mechanical screens to look for investments— that, to me, was always kind of elegant, because it just seemed so logical and reasonable, but there was always something in the back of my mind.

When you looked at a company, you said, "Well, it earned a dollar this year and I am going to muddle it out at 10 percent growth going on for X period of time." Whenever I was doing something, there was something in the back of my mind that always said, but what if it doesn't? I think that that is one of the core attributes of value investors.

If you think about the stock market, the stock market is an exercise in optimism. It is almost an irrational optimism because you are saying whenever you buy something, that you are smarter than the rest of the market. You know more. You have better insight than 100 million people who are willing to buy or sell stocks. I think that is a pretty bold statement for a lot of people. It is a bold statement for everybody.

So to come into what is an optimistic pursuit and be pessimistic about whatever you are looking at, I think it is a pretty interesting mindset, but I don't know that I have seen too many people in the stock market get in trouble by being too pessimistic. Generally speaking, you see the other side of the coin. People say, "Well, this company is growing at 40 percent, it is going to keep growing at 40 percent, or if I want to be conservative about it, it is going to just grow at 36 percent." Well you know, what if it doesn't? What happens then? What is your protection?

I think that that is really the essence of a value investor—someone who enters into situations where he sees, even if he happens to be wrong because it's not like value investors have some greater insight on the future, but they see some sort of defensive stance, be it just in the utterly low level of the stock price, or there is something about the company that they think people are missing. But you still go through the process of being a pessimistic optimist, I guess would be the least awful way to put it.

Buffett reads a whole lot and consumes a ton of information. What are some things that you read on a regular basis, and along those same lines, do you have a couple of books on investing that have been particularly helpful to you?

I do something that Buffett also does, which is that I try to read company annual reports every single day. It can be boring. It can be incredibly tedious going through annual reports of companies that make fasteners for doors for trailer homes and things of that nature. So much of investing I think for a lot of people is received wisdom as opposed to going to the source documents. That, to me, is important. There is an advantage of going there over listening to a Wall Street analyst or something similar. That makes up a huge amount of my day.

I also like reading trade journals. We will get *Quick-Serve Restaurant Monthly* and *Oil Refinery Weekly* and the *Viatical Journal*, for instance.

What was that last one?

Viaticals.

What is a "viatical"?

A "viatical" is when you've got a life insurance policy and you are not yet dead, but you think you would like to trade in the value of that insurance policy. There are companies called viaticals that basically will do that. They will pass you out of your insurance.

But I don't have to die for them to do that, do I?

The good news is you don't have to die. The bad news is you don't get as much money. Someone doesn't get as much money as they would have if you were actually dead.

Hmmm. Got it.

As you can imagine, that is awfully chipper reading, because it has got two of the greatest subjects in the world—it has got death and it has got insurance. That is a cheerful read.

What about investing books?

Both of Joel Greenblatt's books have been incredibly valuable. One is the very modestly titled *You Can Be a Stock Market Genius*, and the other, almost equally modestly titled *The Little Book That Beats the Market*. Both are just spectacular in terms of thinking and in terms of really instructing enterprising investors to some of the oddball places where you can go and find value.

Then obviously the one that you will hear from everyone, and the one that you would hear from Buffett himself would be *Security Analysis* by Benjamin Graham, which I would call the most actively avoided investing book in history, just because it is such hard reading. It is hard reading and it spells almost a puritanical approach to the market that for folks who are optimists, doesn't seem like a whole heck of a lot of fun. It is like taking the joy out of things, but it is truly a wonderful instruction manual for people who want to be value investors.

Aside from Buffett, are there other investors that you have admired for years and learned from and if so, what are some of the key things that you have learned from them?

I mentioned Joel Greenblatt earlier. I think what is great about Joel is that he is someone who, unlike Buffett, who is often buying whole companies at this point, is generally speaking, involved in the market. He has really given an instruction manual for how to think about certain oddball securities that aren't where everyone is looking. Like preferred securities and debt and convertibles and really, really fun things like that, and by "fun" I mean not fun. So yeah, he has been a very important influence.

I think David Nierenberg is probably someone who not everyone will mention. He runs a very concentrated value fund based just outside of Portland, Oregon, in Washington state. I had the opportunity to sit down with them not that long ago, and the thing that they say that I think is a very important thing for investors is they do everything they can to get to know a company. They know the suppliers. They know when the CEO's mother's birthday is. No amount of information to them is too small or too esoteric and they run a very concentrated portfolio and they have done extraordinarily well over time, really based on their willingness to go and try to get an informational edge in an entirely legal way.

It is not like they are trading on insider information or

stealing pitch signals. They just decided that if they are going to invest their money into companies, they are going to know the companies cold. The day they invest is really when the work begins. They think that is a really, really important thing for investors, because so many people, they buy something and say, "Well, time to look for the next thing," and they kind of forget that they just put thousands of dollars into the last thing, and that last thing doesn't stop evolving simply because they have stopped analyzing. That was a really, really valuable thing for me, particularly as we launched the Independence Fund, to just see someone who really walks that walk.

Buffett is known for staying within his circle of competence. Is that an investing trait that you share with him?

It is, though I would say that we try to. I do have a team that works with me and so we have put each person within their own circles of competence and then I depend somewhat upon them to be right, if you will. Our portfolio is not as concentrated as the average, even the collection of companies at Berkshire Hathaway, and it does go across industries and go across geographic boundaries in a way that his does not, but I would say that the circle of competence can be drawn a number of different ways. I know for a fact that I have absolutely no ability to determine either what technology is going to be the next big thing or what drugs have the best chance of succeeding.

So the single-drug biotech companies and then tech companies in general are ones that I just know to stay away from, and not because there aren't opportunities there, but I have no informational advantage. I have no knowledge advantage and basically I would be rolling the dice with received knowledge, and who knows what agenda might be behind that information or the propagator of the information. So I know well enough to stay away from lots of things. I think my wife would probably say that I have no ability to forecast any trends in any walk of life, so that is probably best that I stay away from trying to do so.

What advice do you have for beginning investors?

They say that so many guitar players really burn out because they try to emulate Jimi Hendrix and so many drummers burn out because they try to emulate Neil Peart, and I think that there is something to be said about not trying to be someone else. To being true to yourself and not trying to emulate even someone who is as spectacular as Warren Buffett. He can divide complex fractions in his head. He is really a talent without compare. He is kind of an island unto himself.

I think a lot of people just really try to be the next Buffett instead of trying to be the first whoever they are. Investing is hard enough without saying, "Well, my instinct says X, but Warren Buffett says Y, so I am going to do Y." I think that is a very important thing for people who are just starting out.

My second piece of advice would be to take your time. There is no rush. So many times with beginning investors they get awfully excited about it and before they have studied it for six months, they own 20 different things with 95 percent of their money, and that is scary. It is scary because they might not think it is scary. So take your time, be yourself. That sounds like an after-school special, but it applies.

FURTHER READING: BOOKS FOR INVESTORS OF ALL LEVELS WHO WANT TO LEARN MORE (COURTESY OF *MOTLEY FOOL INSIDE VALUE*)

Four books every aspiring value investor should read:

The Essays of Warren Buffett: Lessons for Corporate America, by Warren E. Buffett and Lawrence A. Cunningham

The Intelligent Investor: A Book of Practical Counsel, by Benjamin Graham

Common Stocks and Uncommon Profits, by Philip A. Fisher

The Little Book That Builds Wealth, by Pat Dorsey

Beginning Investors

Against the Gods: The Remarkable Story of Risk, by Peter L. Bernstein

A Random Walk Down Wall Street, by Burton G. Malkiel

Beating the Street, by Peter Lynch

Buffettology, by Mary Buffett and David Clark

Good to Great: Why Some Companies Make the Leap . . . and Others Don't, by Jim Collins

How to Be a Value Investor, by Lisa Holton

How to Read a Financial Report, by John A. Tracy

Investment Madness: How Psychology Affects Your Investing . . . and What to Do About It, by John R. Nofsinger

One Up on Wall Street: How to Use What You Already Know to Make Money in the Market, by Peter Lynch and John Rothchild

Select Winning Stocks Using Financial Statements, by Richard Loth

The Essential Buffett: Timeless Principles for the New Economy, by Robert G. Hagstrom, Jr.

The Future for Investors: Why the Tried and the True Triumph Over the Bold and the New, by Jeremy J. Siegel

The Little Book of Value Investing, by Christopher H. Browne

The Little Book That Beats the Market, by Joel Greenblatt

The Motley Fool Investment Guide: How the Fool Beats Wall Street's Wise Men and How You Can Too, by David Gardner and Tom Gardner

The Neatest Little Guide to Stock Market Investing, by Jason Kelly

Intermediate Investors

Beyond Greed and Fear: Understanding Behavioral Finance and the Psychology of Investing, by Hersh Shefrin

Buffett: The Making of an American Capitalist, by Roger Lowenstein

Bull's Eye Investing: Targeting Real Returns in a Smoke and Mirrors Market, by John Mauldin

Contrarian Investment Strategies: The Next Generation, by David Dreman

How to Pick Stocks Like Warren Buffett: Profiting from the Value

Hunting Strategies of the World's Most Famous Value Investor, by Timothy Vick

Investing: The Last Liberal Art, by Robert G. Hagstrom

Investment Fables: Exposing the Myths of "Can't Miss" Investment Strategies, by Aswath Damodaran

It's Earnings That Count: Finding Stocks with Earnings Power for Long-Term Profits, by Hewitt Heiserman, Jr.

John Neff on Investing, by John Neff and S. L. Mintz

Just One Thing: Twelve of the World's Best Investors Reveal the One Strategy You Can't Overlook, by John Mauldin

Lessons from the Legends of Wall Street, by Nikki Ross

Money Masters of Our Time, by John Train

More Than You Know: Finding Financial Wisdom in Unconventional Places, by Michael J. Mauboussin

Mosaic: Perspectives on Investing, by Mohnish Pabrai

Poor Charlie's Almanack: The Wit and Wisdom of Charles T. Munger, by Charles T. Munger

The Dhandho Investor: The Low-Risk Value Method to High Returns, by Mohnish Pabrai

The Essential Buffett: Timeless Principles for the New Economy, by Robert G. Hagstrom

The 5 Keys to Value Investing, by J. Dennis Jean-Jacques

The Five Rules for Successful Stock Investing: Morningstar's Guide to Building Wealth and Winning in the Market, by Pat Dorsey

The Focus Investor, by Richard M. Rockwood

The Warren Buffett Portfolio: Mastering the Power of the Focus Investment Strategy, by Robert G. Hagstrom

Value Investing: A Balanced Approach, by Martin J. Whitman

Value Investing: From Graham to Buffett and Beyond, by Bruce C. N. Greenwald, Judd Kahn, Paul D. Sonkin, and Michael van Biema

Value Investing Today, by Charles H. Brandes

When Genius Failed: The Rise and Fall of Long-Term Capital Management, by Roger Lowenstein

You Can Be a Stock Market Genius: Uncover the Secret Hiding Places of Stock Market Profits, by Joel Greenblatt

Advanced Investors

Creative Cash Flow Reporting: Uncovering Sustainable Financial Performance, by Charles W. Mulford and Eugene E. Comiskey

Expectations Investing: Reading Stock Prices for Better Returns, by Alfred Rappaport and Michael J. Mauboussin

Financial Fine Print: Uncovering a Company's True Value, by Michelle Leder

Financial Shenanigans: How to Detect Accounting Gimmicks and Fraud in Financial Reports, by Howard M. Schilit

Financial Warnings, by Charles W. Mulford and Eugene E. Comiskey

Fooled by Randomness: The Hidden Role of Chance in Life and in the Markets, by Nassim Nicholas Taleb

Investment Philosophies: Successful Investment Philosophies and the Greatest Investors Who Made Them Work, by Aswath Damodaran

Investment Valuation: Tools and Techniques for Determining the Value of Any Asset, by Aswath Damodaran

Options as a Strategic Investment, by Lawrence G. McMillan

Quality of Earnings: The Investor's Guide to How Much Money a Company Is Really Making, by Thornton L. O'Glove

Security Analysis: The Classic 1940 Second Edition, by Benjamin Graham and David Dodd

The Aggressive Conservative Investor, by Martin J. Whitman and
   Martin Shubik
The Interpretation of Financial Statements, by Benjamin Graham
   and Spencer B. Meredith
*The (Mis)behavior of Markets: A Fractal View of Risk, Ruin, and
   Reward*, by Benoit Mandelbrot and Richard Hudson
The Quest for Value, by G. Bennett Stewart, III
The Theory of Investment Value, by John Burr Williams
Valuation: Measuring and Managing the Value of Companies, by
   Tim Koller, Marc Goedhart, and David Wessels

Acknowledgments

Funny how things turn out, isn't it? The idea for this book and the initial pitch for it happened way back in the summer of 2007. At the time, we Fools were simply marveling over the studies that had come out of the world of behavioral economics, showing that women and men tended to invest in very different ways. And we noticed something interesting—namely, that it appeared women invested with a very "Buffett-like" temperament. We'd long admired Mr. Buffett and his calm, patient, unflappable temperament. We saw this exemplary temperament as a defining characteristic and an explanation for his ability to build great wealth and beat the market over decades, putting charlatan after charlatan on Wall Street to shame. We knew the importance that Buffett himself placed on investors having the proper temperament, and we believed that by focusing our efforts for this book on uncovering and highlighting the keys to having the optimal temperament, we could help improve the long-term returns of all investors, men and women alike.

What we couldn't have foreseen in our absolute worst nightmares was what was to come for the financial world a little over a year later. As it turned out, we all needed a lesson in temperament, perhaps more than ever before.

Of course, given the choice between watching numerous examples of temperament-gone-wrong unfold before our eyes and *not* having to see our portfolios and nest eggs absolutely demolished, I'm pretty sure we'd have chosen to skip the examples. But here we are, with an eye to the future, and, hopefully, you feel ready to face it with a steady, calm temperament. In fact, you, dear reader, are the first thank-you of many I must make here. Thank you for coming on this journey with me, and for reading this far (you didn't just skip ahead, did you?!). I hope I've made it worth your while, and that you've learned and laughed along the way.

Thank you to Warren Buffett, for modeling the ideal temperament over decades and decades. Thanks, too, for so openly sharing your wisdom with investors everywhere over the years, and for (hopefully!) having a sense of humor about this book's title.

Thank you to David Gardner, Tom Gardner, and Erik Rydholm for founding The Motley Fool oh so many years ago. It's good to be a Fool. Thank you for making it possible and for giving me so many incredible opportunities over the years. And Tom, a special thank-you to you for writing the foreword, for trumpeting this project the whole way through, and for your friendship.

Thank you to Suzanne Gluck, our agent at William Morris Endeavor, for negotiating our book deal and for supporting The Motley Fool every step of the way.

Thank you to my editor at Harper Business, Hollis Heimbouch, for her constant encouragement, sharp edits, thoughtful suggestions, and enormous doses of patience and flexibility. Thank you, Hollis, as well, for your kindness and sense of humor. I couldn't have asked for a better editor and will remain forever grateful.

Thank you also to the other excellent folks at Harper-Collins for being as enthusiastic about this book as we are, including Kathy Schneider, Doug Jones, Angie Lee, Tina Andreadis, Samantha Choy, Mark Ferguson, Matthew Inman, and Colleen Lawrie. It's wonderful to work with a team of people as excited about something as you are!

Thank you to Robyn Gearey, who found the time to make sure this book actually came together while also working triple time to oversee the launch of several new Fool newsletter services. Robyn, thank you for talking me through moments of existential angst, self-confidence swoons, and general freak-outs. Your calm demeanor and encouraging manner were a godsend. Thank you for always being there.

Thank you to money managers Lisa Rapuano, Lauren Templeton, Candace King Weir, Amelia Weir, and Bill Mann for taking the time out of their packed schedules to do interviews for this book. Thank you for sharing your experiences with all of us.

Thank you to Fools Mac Greer, Chris Hill, and Steve Broido for all their help nailing down interviews and quotes from folks like Roger Lowenstein, Andrew Kilpatrick, Prem Jain, and Nell Minow. Word to the wise: if you need to talk to anybody (seriously, just about anybody), these are the three guys who can pull it off.

Thank you to Fools John Reeves and Alex Pape for fact-checking this book within an inch of its life and for their excellent overall comments on the manuscript. Thank you both for saving me from my mistakes! Thank you also to Fools Hope Nelson, Paul Elliott, Todd Etter, Buck Hartzell, and Andy Cross for reading the manuscript and sharing your ideas on how to make it as good as it could possibly be. All of your suggestions were enormously helpful. Thank you all for taking the time to work on this when I know you had about a million other things going on at the same time.

Thank you to the Fool's own marketing guru, the aforementioned Paul Elliott, and to the Fool's public relations guru, Alison Southwick, for never shooting down a crazy idea and for their willingness to go all out to make this book a hit. Thank you to Fool Dan Stapleton for working his design magic on the cover. Thanks to Fools Ginni Bratti and Randy Coon for supporting this project. Thank you to Fool writers Alyce Lomax and Dayana Yochim for being such inspirations. Thanks to Joe Magyer and the entire *Motley Fool Inside Value* team for so graciously sharing their reading list. And thank you to Fool Jonathan Mudd for pulling one sentence buried within a book proposal to the forefront, thereby giving us our most excellent book title.

Last, but certainly not in any way least, thanks to Austin for your love and support as I sat hunched over my laptop, pecking away on this for seemingly days and nights on end. Thanks for making me laugh and smile when I needed it (a lot). Thanks for being sweet and understanding and patient. Thanks for making me endless cups of tea and pots of coffee. Thanks for distracting me with episodes of *The Office* just when I thought I'd reached my breaking point and needed some levity from that titan of the paper business himself, Michael Scott. Mostly, thanks for putting up with me. I appreciate it, and am more grateful for you than I can express. Thank you.

Notes

1: Why Temperament Matters Now More Than Ever

1. Todd Wenning, "The Wall Street Panic of 2008," The Motley Fool, http://www.fool.com/investing/general/the-wall-street-panic-of-2008.aspx.
2. Andrew Ross Sorkin, *Too Big to Fail* (New York: Penguin, 2010), 10.
3. Warren E. Buffett, Berkshire Hathaway 2007 Shareholder Letter, February 2008, http://www.berkshirehathaway.com/letters/2007ltr.pdf, 3.
4. *The American Heritage Dictionary*, 4th ed., s.v. "temperament."
5. Warren Boronson, *J. K. Lasser's Pick Stocks Like Warren Buffett* (New York: Wiley, 2001), 246.
6. *BusinessWeek,* July 5, 1999, quoted in Robert G. Hagstrom, *The Warren Buffett Way,* 2nd ed. (Hoboken, NJ: Wiley, 2005), 178.
7. Sheelah Kolhatkar, "What if Women Ran Wall Street?," *New York*, March 21, 2010, http://nymag.com/news/businessfinance/64950/.
8. Sorkin, *Too Big to Fail*, 29.
9. Michael Lewis, "Wall Street on the Tundra," *Vanity Fair*, April 2009.
10. Ruth Sunderland, "After the crash, Iceland's women lead the rescue," *Observer*, February 22, 2009, http://www.guardian.co.uk/world/2009/feb/22/iceland-women.
11. David Jolly, "Iceland Emerged from Recession in 3rd Quarter," *New York Times*, December 7, 2010, http://www.nytimes.com/2010/12/08/business/global/08icecon.html.

2: The Science Behind the Girl

1. Hanna Rosin, "The End of Men," *Atlantic*, July/August 2010, http://www
   .theatlantic.com/magazine/archive/2010/07/the-end-of-men/8135/.
2. Ibid.
3. Daniel de Vise, "Report: More women than men in U.S. earned doctorates
   last year for first time," *Washington Post*, September 14, 2010, http://www
   .washingtonpost.com/wp-dyn/content/article/2010/09/14/AR201009
   1400004.html.
4. Rosin, "The End of Men."
5. Brad M. Barber and Terrance Odean, "Boys Will Be Boys: Gender, Overconfidence, and Common Stock Investment," *Quarterly Journal of Economics*
   116, no. 1 (February 2001), 261–92.
6. John Ameriks, Ph.D., Jill Marshall, and Liqian Ren, Ph.D., "Equity aban-
   donment in 2008–2009: Lower among balanced fund investors," Vanguard,
   https://institutional.vanguard.com/iam/pdf/RPD25.pdf, December 2009.
7. Joan MacLeod Heminway, "Female Investors and Securities Fraud: Is the
   Reasonable Investor a Woman?," University of Tennessee at Knoxville College of Law, Legal Studies Research Paper Series, research paper 77, October 2009.
8. Stefan Ruenzi and Alexandra Niessen, "Sex Matters: Gender Differences in
   the Mutual Fund Industry," http://ssrn.com/abstract=1343490, February
   15, 2009.
9. Ibid.
10. "50 Leading Women in Hedge Funds: A report in association with Price
    Waterhouse Coopers," *Hedge Fund Journal*, February 2010, http://www.the
    hedgefundjournal.com/magazine/201002/research/thfj-50-women-in
    -hedge-funds.pdf.
11. "Women in Fund Management: A Road Map for Achieving Critical
    Mass—and Why It Matters," National Council for Research on Women,
    August 2009, http://www.ncrw.org/sites/ncrw.org/files/WIFM%20Report
    .pdf.
12. "When It Comes to Investing, Gender a Strong Influence on Behavior,"
    Merrill Lynch Investment Managers, April 18, 2005.
13. Claremont Graduate University Media Services, http://www.cgu.edu
    /pages/4627.asp.
14. Jason Palmer, "Traders' raging hormones cause stock market swings," *New
    Scientist*, April 14, 2008, http://www.newscientist.com/article/dn13664
    -traders-raging-hormones-cause-stock-market-swings.html.

15. John M. Coates, Mark Gurnell, and Zoltan Sarnyai, "From molecule to market: Steroid hormones and financial risk-taking," *Philosophical Transactions of the Royal Society: Biological Sciences*, January 27, 2010.
16. Ibid.
17. Ibid.
18. Ibid.

3: A Quick Intro to the Oracle

1. Warren Buffett, interview with Liz Claman, "The Billionaire Next Door," CNBC, December 2006.
2. Alice Schroeder, *The Snowball: Warren Buffett and the Business of Life* (New York: Bantam, 2009), 88.
3. John Train, *The Money Masters* (New York: HarperCollins, 1994), 16.
4. Lauren Templeton, interview with author, September 22, 2010, published as transcribed.
5. Schroeder, *The Snowball*, 148–49.
6. Alex Crippen, "CNBC Transcript: Warren Buffett's $200B Berkshire Blunder and the Valuable Lesson He Learned," October 18, 2010, http://www.cnbc.com/id/39724884.

4: Trade Less, Make More

1. Warren E. Buffett, Berkshire Hathaway 1988 Shareholder Letter, February 28, 1989, http://www.berkshirehathaway.com/letters/1988.html.
2. David A. Vise and Steve Coll, "Salomon Deal Generates More Buffett-Watching," *Washington Post*, September 30, 1987.
3. Jennifer Myers, "28 Business, Investment, Academic & Labor Leaders Join Aspen Institute in Bold Call to Overcome Short-Termism," Aspen Institute press release, September 9, 2009, http://www.aspeninstitute.org /news/2009/09/09/28-business-investment-academic-labor-leaders-join -aspen-institute-bold-call-overcom.
4. Warren E. Buffett, "An Owner's Manual," 1996, http://www.berkshire hathaway.com/ownman.pdf, 1.
5. Mark Hulbert, "Be a Tiger Not a Hen," *Forbes*, May 25, 1992, quoted in Hagstrom, *The Warren Buffett Way*, 180.
6. Warren Buffett, 1992 Berkshire Hathaway annual meeting, quoted in Janet Lowe, *Warren Buffett Speaks: Wit and Wisdom from the World's Greatest Investor* (Hoboken, NJ: Wiley, 2007), 163–64.

7. ———, Berkshire Hathaway 1996 Shareholder Letter, quoted in Warren E. Buffett and Lawrence Cunningham, *The Essays of Warren Buffett*, 2nd ed. (New York: Cunningham Group, 2008), 108.

8. Prem Jain, email interview with Mac Greer of The Motley Fool, September 27, 2010.

9. Matt Logan, "Buying the Buffett Way," The Motley Fool, March 26, 2003, http://www.fool.com/news/2003/03/26/buying-the-buffett-way.aspx.

10. Murray Chass, "Buffett Is Invested in Rodriguez," *New York Times*, August 10, 2007, http://www.nytimes.com/2007/08/10/sports/baseball/10chass.html.

11. Lisa Rapuano, interview with author, September 10, 2010, published as transcribed.

12. Tom and David Gardner, *Million Dollar Portfolio* (New York: Harper Collins, 2009), xiii.

13. Morgan Housel, "Learn from Buffett's Patience," The Motley Fool, November 20, 2008, http://www.fool.com/investing/value/2008/11/20/learn-from-buffetts-patience.aspx.

14. Warren E. Buffett, Berkshire Hathaway 1986 Shareholder Letter, quoted in Buffett and Cunningham, *The Essays of Warren Buffett*, 2nd ed., 95.

5: Rein in Overconfidence

1. Warren E. Buffett, Buffett Partnership, Ltd., Letter to Partners, January 25, 1967, http://www.pragcap.com/wp-content/uploads/2010/02/BP20.pdf.

2. Warren Buffett and Carol Loomis, "Mr. Buffett on the Stock Market," *Fortune*, November 22, 1999, http://money.cnn.com/magazines/fortune/fortune_archive/1999/11/22/269071/index.htm.

3. Schroeder, *The Snowball*, 277.

4. Buffett, Buffett Partnership, Ltd., Letter to Partners, January 25, 1967.

5. Lauren Templeton, interview with author, September 22, 2010, published as transcribed.

6. Warren E. Buffett, Berkshire Hathaway 1982 Shareholder Letter, http://www.berkshirehathaway.com/letters/1982.html.

6: Shun Risk

1. Warren E. Buffett, Berkshire Hathaway 1992 Shareholder Letter, in Buffett and Cunningham, *The Essays of Warren Buffett*, 2nd ed., 103.

2. Lowe, *Warren Buffett Speaks*, p. 116.

3. Warren E. Buffett, Berkshire Hathaway 1985 Shareholder Letter, in Buffett and Cunningham, *The Essays of Warren Buffett*, 2nd ed., 77.

4. ———, Berkshire Hathaway 2008 Shareholder Letter, February 27, 2009, http://www.berkshirehathaway.com/letters/2008ltr.pdf, 16.

7: Focus on the Positives of Pessimism

1. Warren E. Buffett, "Buy American. I Am," op-ed, *New York Times*, October 16, 2008, http://www.nytimes.com/2008/10/17/opinion/17buffett.html.

2. Ibid.

3. Ibid.

4. ———, Berkshire Hathaway 2008 Shareholder Letter, 5.

5. ———, Berkshire Hathaway 2009 Shareholder Letter, February 26, 2010, http://www.berkshirehathaway.com/letters/2009ltr.pdf, 15.

6. Benjamin Graham, *The Intelligent Investor*, revised ed. (New York: Harper Collins, 2006), 204–5.

7. Warren E. Buffett, "You Pay a Very High Price in the Stock Market for a Cheery Consensus," *Forbes*, August 6, 1979, republished at Forbes.com on November 8, 2008, http://www.forbes.com/2008/11/08/buffett-forbes -article-markets-cx_pm-1107stocks.html.

8. Bill Mann, interview with Chris Hill of The Motley Fool, September 22, 2010, published as transcribed.

8: Research Extensively

1. Schroeder, *The Snowball*, 173.

2. Ibid.

3. Ibid., 149.

4. Roger Lowenstein, *Buffett: The Making of an American Capitalist* (New York: Random House, 2008), 32, 287.

5. Schroeder, *The Snowball*, 445.

6. Lowenstein, *Buffett*, 150.

7. Quoted by Peter Lynch, Foreword to the first edition of *The Warren Buffett Way*, in Hagstrom, *The Warren Buffett Way*, 2nd ed., x.

8. Andrew Kilpatrick, email interview with Mac Greer of The Motley Fool, September 22, 2010.

9. Lisa Rapuano, interview with author, September 10, 2010, published as transcribed.

10. Jason Zweig, "How to Ignore the Yes-Man in Your Head," *Wall Street*

Journal, November 19, 2009, http://online.wsj.com/article/SB10001424052
74870381160457453368003777 8184.html.
11. Buffett, Berkshire Hathaway 2008 Shareholder Letter, 16.
12. Ibid.

9: Ignore Peer Pressure

1. Warren E. Buffett, Buffett Partnership, Ltd., Letter·to Partners, January 25, 1967, http://www.pragcap.com/wp-content/uploads/2010/02/BP20.pdf.
2. Warren E. Buffett and Bill Gates, interview by Becky Quick, "Warren Buffett and Bill Gates: Keeping America Great," CNBC, November 22, 2009.
3. Buffett, Buffett Partnership, Ltd., Letter to Partners, January 25, 1967.
4. Warren E. Buffett, "Look at All Those Beautiful, Scantily Clad Girls Out There!," *Forbes*, November 1, 1974, republished at Forbes.com on April 20, 2008, http://www.forbes.com/2008/04/30/warren-buffett-profile-invest-oped -cx_hs_0430buffett.html.
5. Mac Greer, "The Most Underrated Part of Warren Buffett's Success," The Motley Fool, July 19, 2010, http://www.fool.com/investing/gen eral/2010/07/19/the-most-underrated-part-of-warren-buffetts-succes.aspx.
6. Roger Lowenstein, email interview with Mac Greer of The Motley Fool, September 16, 2010.
7. Candace King Weir, interview with author, October 7, 2010, published as transcribed.
8. Jason Zweig, "So That's Why Investors Can't Think for Themselves," *Wall Street Journal Online*, June 19, 2010, http://online.wsj.com/article/SB100014 24052748703438604575314932570154178.html.
9. Buffett, Berkshire Hathaway 2008 Shareholder Letter, 16.
10. Schroeder, *The Snowball*, 133–34.
11. Andy Serwer, "The Oracle of Everything," *Fortune*, November 11, 2002, http://money.cnn.com/magazines/fortune/fortune_archive/2002 /11/11/331843/index.htm.
12. Lisa Rapuano, interview with author, September 10, 2010, published as transcribed.
13. Schroeder, *The Snowball*, 698.
14. Buffett, "Buy American."
15. Lowenstein, *Buffett*, 133.
16. Ibid., 111.
17. Schroeder, *The Snowball*, 31–32.

10: Learn from Mistakes

1. Jason Zweig, "What Warren Buffett Wants You to Know," *Money*, May 3, 2004, http://money.cnn.com/2004/05/03/pf/buffett_qanda/.
2. Warren E. Buffett, Berkshire Hathaway 1996 Shareholder Letter, in Buffett and Cunningham, *The Essays of Warren Buffett*, 2nd ed., 134.
3. ———, Berkshire Hathaway 1994 Shareholder Letter, in Buffett and Cunningham, *The Essays of Warren Buffett*, 2nd ed., 132.
4. ———, Berkshire Hathaway 1996 Shareholder Letter, in Buffett and Cunningham, *The Essays of Warren Buffett*, 2nd ed., 134.
5. Lowenstein, *Buffett*, 354.
6. Warren E. Buffett, Berkshire Hathaway 2007 Shareholder Letter, February 2008, http://www.berkshirehathaway.com/letters/2007ltr.pdf, 8.
7. ———, Berkshire Hathaway 2009 Shareholder Letter, February 26, 2010, http://www.berkshirehathaway.com/letters/2009ltr.pdf, 12.
8. Schroeder, *The Snowball*, 593.
9. Ibid., 252.
10. Lisa Rapuano, interview with author, September 10, 2010, published as transcribed.
11. Warren E. Buffett, Berkshire Hathaway 2008 Shareholder Letter, February 27, 2009, http://www.berkshirehathaway.com/letters/2008ltr.pdf, 16.
12. Ibid.
13. Warren E. Buffett, Berkshire Hathaway 1989 Shareholder Letter, March 2, 1990, http://www.berkshirehathaway.com/letters/1989.html.

11: Embrace Feminine Influences

1. Schroeder, *The Snowball*, 281.
2. Sam Whiting, "The Bridge Club: What Do Sharon Osberg, Warren Buffett and Bill Gates Share? A love of bridge," SFGate.com, January 22, 2006, http://articles.sfgate.com/2006-01-22/living/17278374_1_bill-gates-mr-buffett-bridge.
3. "Like a Marriage, Only More Enduring," *Magazine from The Wall Street Journal*, December 2, 2010, http://magazine.wsj.com/people-ideas/partnership/like-a-marriage-only-more-enduring/.
4. Katharine Graham, *Personal History* (New York: Vintage, 1998), 525.
5. Washington Post Company, "Warren Buffett to Retire from the Board of The Washington Post Company," January 20, 2011, http://finance.yahoo.com/news/Warren-Buffett-to-Retire-from-bw-3922745384.html.

6. Liz Claman, "Buffett: Wouldn't buy more newspapers at any price," May 2, 2009, http://liz.blogs.foxbusiness.com/2009/05/02/buffett-wouldnt-buy-more-newspapers-at-any-price/.

7. Washington Post Company, "Warren Buffett to Retire."

8. Warren E. Buffett, Berkshire Hathaway 1983 Shareholder Letter, March 14, 1984, http://www.berkshirehathaway.com/letters/1983.html.

9. ————, Berkshire Hathaway 1984 Shareholder Letter, February 25, 1985, http://www.berkshirehathaway.com/letters/1984.html.

10. ————, Berkshire Hathaway 2007 Shareholder Letter, 13.

11. Ibid.

12: Maintain Consistent, Persistent Results

1. Train, *The Money Masters*, 1.

2. Warren E. Buffett, "The Superinvestors of Graham-and-Doddsville," in Graham, *The Intelligent Investor*, rev. ed., appendix 1, 537.

3. Ibid., 546.

4. Warren E. Buffett, Berkshire Hathaway 1988 Shareholder Letter, in Buffett and Cunningham, *The Essays of Warren Buffett*, 2nd ed., 88–89.

5. ————, Berkshire Hathaway 2009 Shareholder Letter, February 26, 2010, http://www.berkshirehathaway.com/letters/2009ltr.pdf, 4.

13: Value People and Relationships

1. Schroeder, *The Snowball*, 273.

2. Warren E. Buffett, Berkshire Hathaway 1989 Shareholder Letter, March 2, 1990, http://www.berkshirehathaway.com/letters/1989.html.

3. Nell Minow, interview with Chris Hill of The Motley Fool, September 22, 2010.

4. Warren E. Buffett, "An Owner's Manual," 1996, http://www.berkshirehathaway.com/ownman.pdf, 5.

5. Prem Jain, email interview with Mac Greer of The Motley Fool, September 27, 2010.

6. Lisa Rapuano, interview with author, September 10, 2010, published as transcribed.

7. Amelia Weir, interview with author, October 7, 2010, published as transcribed.

8. Michael D. Eisner, with Aaron Cohen, *Working Together: Why Great Partnerships Succeed* (New York: Harper Business, 2010), 35–36.

9. Lowenstein, *Buffett*, 75.

10. Eisner and Cohen, *Working Together*, 36.

11. Schroeder, *The Snowball*, 532.

12. Carol Loomis, "Warren Buffett gives it away," *Fortune*, July 10, 2006, http://money.cnn.com/magazines/fortune/fortune_archive/2006/07/10/8380864/index.htm.

13. Carol Loomis, "The $600 billion challenge," *Fortune*, June 16, 2010, http://features.blogs.fortune.cnn.com/2010/06/16/gates-buffett-600-billion-dollar-philanthropy-challenge/.

14. Hagstrom, *The Warren Buffett Way*, 167.

15. Lowenstein, *Buffett*, 45.

16. Warren E. Buffett, Berkshire Hathaway 1986 Shareholder Letter, in Buffett and Cunningham, *The Essays of Warren Buffett*, 2nd ed., 50.

14: Question the Masters

1. Warren E. Buffett, Berkshire Hathaway 1992 Shareholder Letter, in Buffett and Cunningham, *The Essays of Warren Buffett*, 2nd ed., 103.

2. Schroeder, *The Snowball*, 221

3. Philip A. Fisher, *Common Stocks and Uncommon Profits* (New York: Wiley, 1996), 16–19.

4. Warren E. Buffett, Berkshire Hathaway 1989 Shareholder Letter, March 2, 1990, http://www.berkshirehathaway.com/letters/1989.html.

5. ——, Berkshire Hathaway 1993 Shareholder letter, in Buffett and Cunningham, *The Essays of Warren Buffett*, 2nd ed., 90–91.

6. Schroeder, *The Snowball*, 133–34.

15: Act Fairly and Ethically

1. Alyce Lomax, "Pop the Champagne! RegFD Turns 10," The Motley Fool, August 11, 2010, http://www.fool.com/investing/general/2010/08/11/pop-the-champagne-regfd-turns-10.aspx.

2. Warren E. Buffett, Berkshire Hathaway 2000 Shareholder Letter, in Buffett and Cunningham, *The Essays of Warren Buffett*, 2nd ed., 38.

3. Warren E. Buffett, "An Owner's Manual," 1996, http://www.berkshirehathaway.com/ownman.pdf, 4.

4. Ibid.

5. Schroeder, *The Snowball*, 229.

6. Susan Gharib, "Warren and Charlie: Ethics 101," xChange: The NBR Blog, May 3, 2010, http://www.pbs.org/nbr/blog/2010/05/warren_and_charlie _ethics_101.html

16: Foolish Investing Principles 101

1. Andrew Kilpatrick, email interview with Mac Greer of The Motley Fool, September 22, 2010.
2. Lisa Rapuano, interview with author, September 10, 2010, published as transcribed.
3. Candace King Weir, interview with author, October 7, 2010, published as transcribed.
4. Bill Mann, interview with Chris Hill of The Motley Fool, September 22, 2010, published as transcribed.
5. William J. Bernstein, *The Four Pillars of Investing: Lessons for Building a Winning Portfolio* (New York: McGraw-Hill, 2002/2010), 268.
6. Warren E. Buffett, Berkshire Hathaway 2009 Shareholder Letter, February 26, 2010, http://www.berkshirehathaway.com/letters/2009ltr.pdf, 14.
7. The section on selling is pulled, in large part, from Step 10, "Don't Sell Too Soon," in "The Motley Fool's 13 Steps to Investing Foolishly," written by Joe Magyer and Rich Greifner, and found here: http://www.fool.com/how -to-invest/thirteen-steps/index.aspx.

Index